SPHERE RIG

Other titles in the *Sphere Rights Guides* series:

SPHERE RIGHTS GUIDES
Series Editor: Andrew Arden

THE SINGLE PARENTS HANDBOOK

JENNY LEVIN and *FRANCES LOGAN*

SPHERE REFERENCE

A SPHERE BOOK

First published in Great Britain by Sphere Books Ltd 1990
Copyright © Frances Logan and Jenny Levin 1990

Reproduced, printed and bound in Great Britain by
The Guernsey Press

ISBN 0 7474 0211 6

Sphere Books Ltd
A Division of
Macdonald & Co (Publishers) Ltd
27 Wrights Lane, London W8 5TZ

A member of Maxwell Pergamon Publishing Corporation plc

Publisher's Notice

The Law can change at short notice. This book describes the law relating to single parents as at 31st July 1989. You should always check if what it says is still correct.

Contents

Contents

Contents

Contents

A. EMPLOYMENT RIGHTS

Contents

Contents

Can we make an agreement about maintenance?

Contents

Introduction

People often think that families consist of a happily married couple with two children, usually looked after by the mother who stays at home until they are safely at school. In reality, life does not always conform to this stereotype – one in three marriages will probably end in divorce, over 100,000 children each year in England and Wales are born outside marriage. Many married women work outside the home and many people live with others or on their own with children.

This book looks at the law and policy as it affects the one million one-parent families in Great Britain today. It is one of a series of handbooks which aims at providing information in many different areas of the law.

The law affects single parents in relation to housing, welfare benefits, rights over their children, rights in relation to their partner or former partner, employment, nationality and immigration, and child care. Problems can also arise on the death of a partner or parent.

People become part of a 'one-parent family' in many ways. Most single parents are on their own with children as a result of the breakdown of their marriage. They may be divorced or just separated. Some are left on their own after the death of their partner – both within and outside of marriage (widows and widowers have certain particular rights on the death of their spouse). Others are single parents by choice – having decided to have a child on their own, or having decided not to live with the other parent or with anyone else. Some single parents are separated by circumstance – the other parent may be in hospital or prison, or may not be allowed to enter the country because of the way our immigration rules

1

operate, or because of the emigration rules of another country.

Some single parents face particular problems because of age, or sexual orientation or their national origin, or because they have physical or mental disabilities.

Like everyone else, one-parent families live in very different circumstances, but they are united by the general problem of poverty and also by the fact that society still regards them, in some way, as abnormal.

A note on the scope of this book
This handbook is a guide to the law and practice in England and Wales only. The law in Scotland and Northern Ireland may be different in several aspects. It may be useful to contact the following organizations if you want help or information in Scotland or Northern Ireland:

Scotland
Scottish Council for Single Parents,
39 Hope Street,
Glasgow G2 6AE.
Tel: 041-248 3488.
or
13 Gayfield Square,
Edinburgh EH1 3NX.
Tel: 031-556 3899.

Northern Ireland
Gingerbread,
171 University Street,
Belfast.
Tel: 0232-231417.
(a self help group of lone parents)

The law in England and Wales is stated as at April

1989. The law can change quite quickly, so it is important to check with one of the advice agencies listed in Chapter 9 if you think the law may have altered in some way since then.

It is also important to seek further advice if you are under 18 years of age. The law in England and Wales often treats young people under 18 differently from adults, depending on the circumstances and the person's age at the time. Not all the information contained in this handbook may apply in the same way to a single parent under the age of 18.

It is most important that single parents make sure that they know their rights and how to enforce them. This handbook provides some of the answers but each person's circumstances can be quite different and it may be necessary to get further information or advice from an advice agency or solicitor. It is important not to delay in seeking help – generally the earlier help is sought the better. Legal aid may be available for both advice and help in the courts from a solicitor.

This handbook does not deal with the position of couples who are still living with each other. Other books in the series will be of assistance in these areas of the law. Nor does it deal, in any detail, with how to cope with debts. Single parents may face difficulties in paying rent and housing costs, repairs and household items or coping with fuel bills. Often the problems arise when a marriage or relationship breaks down and one partner leaves the other with huge debts. The book gives information about how to increase your income by claiming various benefits or maintenance, but does not set out how to negotiate with fuel boards, credit companies and councils. Chapter 9 will give information on where to go for further help.

As will be obvious, this book brings together a wide variety of laws, rules, guidance, etc. affecting single parents on many issues – housing, money, work, divorce, immigration and so on. No single book can cover all these areas in detail. For more information look at the other titles in this series.

As a single parent you are not alone in facing whatever difficulties are before you. One in seven families is headed by a single parent and many of those single parents have found that the best help and support has come from other single parents – there is often no need to explain the problem or feel awkward as the other person knows exactly what it is like to bring up children alone in this society. There are many single-parent groups round the country and they may be a good place to start.

1: Your Home

A. GETTING A HOME

What can I do if I have nowhere to live?

The local council has a legal obligation to help you if you have nowhere to live or if you are likely to lose your home in the near future. This is laid down in the Housing Act 1985. This does not mean that they always have to give you a home, but that they will have to give you some help in finding somewhere yourself. This 'help' may be giving you a list of hotels in the area which could give you bed and breakfast accommodation, or giving you information about what other help you can get in the area. If you fulfil certain conditions, then the council may be under an obligation to rehouse you. (See below for these conditions.)

What should I do first?

If your housing problem is homelessness, or you are about to become homeless, go to your local council Housing Department. You can ask any council for help. Ask for the person who deals with homeless families. In some councils they have a department called the Homeless Persons Unit or Emergency Housing Unit. You should make sure that the person who sees you knows that you are asking for help because you are homeless or about to be homeless. Do not be fobbed off by being put on the council housing waiting list, or on the transfer list if you are already in council property.

If you have nowhere to stay that night, the Housing Department should arrange overnight accommodation. If the office is closed or you are trying to get help at a weekend, in the evening or at night, there should be an emergency duty officer or social worker who can arrange overnight accommodation. Ring the town hall number or ask at the local police station.

In addition, there may be a local women's aid refuge who can help and who may be able to give you somewhere to stay if you need to leave home because of violence or the risk of violence. The local police should help you contact the local refuge, and other advice agencies in the area will help if they are open. If you cannot get help locally you can contact the head offices of Women's Aid in England and Wales who will put you in contact with a refuge who will be able to help you. See Chapter 9 for details.

What do I have to do to get rehoused by the Council?

The council has a legal obligation to provide you with some form of housing if you are:

    (a) homeless, or threatened with homelessness, *and*
    (b) in 'priority need', *and*
    (c) not become intentionally homeless, *and*
    (d) have a local connection within their area.

All these conditions are described at greater length below.

If you satisfy all these four conditions the Housing Department will either help you return to your old home if that is possible, or, if that is not possible, they will find you somewhere else to live. It probably will not be possible to give you a permanent new home straight away. In all probability you will be offered temporary accommodation until somewhere permanent becomes available. This may mean that you will have to spend some time in a bed and breakfast hotel or a hostel or other temporary home.

This accommodation is often of very poor quality, and you may have to share cooking and washing facilities with many other families. It can be particularly hard having to share one room with your children and not having anywhere else where they can play safely. In some areas, families may remain in some form of temporary accommodation for many months or even years.

If there are particular problems with the temporary accommodation you are in, you should tell the Housing Department and see if there is anywhere else they could put you and your family. However, there is no guarantee that they will be able to put you in anything better.

You will be charged rent for your stay in temporary accommodation, but the amount will normally depend on your financial circumstances.

When will I be accepted as being homeless?

The Council housing department must accept that you are homeless if:

(a) you do not have anywhere you and your children can live together, *or*

(b) although you have a home, you cannot get into it, for example, because you have been thrown out of it by your landlord or your partner, *or*

(c) you have been forced out of your home because of violence or threats of violence from your partner or someone who lives in the home with you.

You should also be accepted as homeless if you are currently living somewhere but are threatened with homelessness. This means that within the next 28 days you are likely to become actually homeless. If you have been told to leave your home by your landlord or your partner, you should get immediate advice on your rights to remain. Before it accepts you as homeless, the Housing Department will want proof that you have no alternative but to leave home. If you rent your home from a private landlord, the landlord may give you a notice to quit or you may be sent a notice of possession proceedings from the local County court. You do not have to leave your home until after the judge in the County court has heard the case and he or she decides you have to go. Do not leave your home without getting advice first. If you leave your home before you have to, it is possible that the Housing Department will not give you anywhere else to live.

Will I count as homeless if I live with relatives or friends?

If you are living with friends or relatives the Housing Department will not regard you as homeless unless your friends say clearly that they want you to leave. The Housing Department may talk to your family or friends or visit them, and may demand that they give you written notice to go. The Housing Department should not insist, however, that your family or friends go to court to get you out.

You should also be treated as being homeless if you live in a mobile home, such as a caravan, and you do not have anywhere to park it and live in it.

It can be very difficult to get help from the Housing Department if you do have somewhere to live but it is in an awful condition or very overcrowded. It will depend on your particular circumstances, but generally if you have a roof over your head then you may not be considered as homeless.

If you are in this situation it is very important that you get advice before you do anything about leaving or you may find that you are treated as being intentionally homeless.

What is my position if I live in a women's refuge?

You should be treated as homeless by the council (provided there is nowhere else you can live). The courts have decided that a women's refuge is simply temporary accommodation which is not suitable for the long-term accommodation of women and their children.

When will I be regarded as in priority need?

You will be considered as in priority need if you are in any of the following circumstances:

(a) you have dependent children living with you, or who would live with you if they could. For example, if you are separated from your children only because you have nowhere to live together, or they are in local authority care until you get somewhere to live, then you will be in priority need.

Children are regarded as being 'dependent' if they are under 16 years or if they are up to 19 years but still in full-time education. You should not be asked to get a custody order. The Housing Department should look at your particular circumstances to see if you have a child dependent on you, *or*

(b) you are pregnant or live with someone who is pregnant. You should be accepted as homeless at any stage in your pregnancy. You should get a certificate of pregnancy from your doctor or hospital to prove it to the housing department, *or*

(c) you are homeless as a result of an emergency such as a fire or flood, *or*

(d) you are 'vulnerable' because of old age, mental illness or handicap or physical disability or other special reason. This generally means that you are less able to look after yourself because of your particular problems. The Housing Department will want medical or other evidence to support your claim. 'Old age' is generally retirement age, but may be younger.

When will I be regarded as intentionally homeless?

If the Housing Department decides that you made yourself homeless through your own actions, or by agreeing to the actions of another, then you will be regarded as intentionally homeless and the Housing Department are not under any obligation to provide you with somewhere else to live. They should, however, give you advice about finding other accommodation. They should also provide you with temporary accommodation for a while, usually about 28 days, to allow you to find somewhere else to live. Once this time is up they will not have to give you anywhere else and it will be up to you to find somewhere to live.

You will not be intentionally homeless if you have been forced to leave your home, e.g. because of violence or a court order, but if you leave your home when you did not have to, you may be declared intentionally homeless. For example, if you leave the home because of violence but failed to use your remedies under the Domestic Violence legislation where appropriate, then you might be declared intentionally homeless.

If you do not pay your rent, or do something else that leads your landlord to take court proceedings to evict you, you may be declared intentionally homeless. However, if the rent was your partner's responsibility and it is in arrears because he or she did not pay it, you should tell this to the Housing Department. Similarly, you should tell the Housing Department if you could not pay the rent because you were not receiving the right housing benefits. In these circumstances you should not be considered homeless through your own fault.

If your home went with your partner's job and he or she gave the job up and you could not prevent it happening, you should not be considered homeless through your own fault. It is very important that you tell the Housing Department exactly why you lost your home or had to leave it. If they say it was your fault or that you are intentionally homeless, get advice quickly. It may be necessary for you to see a solicitor, but it can be difficult to take the Housing Department to court under homelessness legislation.

Which council should I go to?

A council will have an obligation to help you if you have a local connection with it. You will be considered to have a local connection with a local authority area if:

(a) you have lived in the area for six of the last twelve months or for three of the last five years, *or*

(b) you are employed in the area (a short period of employment may not count), *or*

(c) you have close relatives living in the area who have lived there for at least five years, *or*

(d) you have other special circumstances.

Living in a mother and baby home or hospital or being in the armed forces in an area will not usually count as a local connection. Neither will living in married quarters during or after marriage to someone in the armed forces.

If you apply for help to the Housing Department in the area with which you have a local connection, then that Housing Department must help you and cannot refer you anywhere else. If you do not have such a local connection, but do have a local connection in another area then you may be referred to that area.

If you do not have a local connection with any area, then the Housing Department to which you apply must help you.

If you have left home because of violence or threats of violence from your partner, and there is a risk of further violence if you went back to the area you came from, you should not be referred back there unless you are sure it is safe. If the Housing Department tries to send you back, get immediate advice from the local Women's Aid refuge if there is one, or from one of the advice centres in your area.

What can I do about my furniture?

If you need to have your furniture and belongings stored whilst you are homeless or in temporary accommodation, then the Housing Department should help you. They may charge you for doing this, but this will depend on your financial circumstances.

What housing will I be offered if I am homeless?

Most Housing Departments will make one offer only of permanent housing to homeless people. The offer should be suitable for you and your family in terms of area, employment prospects, size, and your wishes, but it need not be in the local authority area itself. In practice, it is very difficult to reject an offer of accommodation unless it is completely unreasonable and unsuitable. It is very important that you get advice before you reject the offer because if you reject an offer without good reason the Housing Department may say that they have discharged their legal duty to you by offering you one place, and may not offer you anywhere else.

You may need help from a local councillor, your doctor, health visitor, social worker if you have one, or anyone who can back up your case as to why you need another offer to be made. The local authority itself may have an appeal process to deal with disputes over offers.

For further information, see *The Homeless Persons Handbook*, published in this series.

What other ways are there to get a home?

It is beyond the scope of this book to provide detailed help on all the possible ways of getting a home. What follows is a summary of the available options. For more detailed information, see *The Public Tenants Handbook*, *The Private Tenants Handbook* and *The Owner-Occupiers Handbook*, all of which are published in this series. Financial benefits in relation to housing costs are dealt with in Chapter 5.

1. Owner-occupation

Buying your own home is very difficult unless you have a regular income from a permanent job and some savings to put down as a deposit. As most one-parent families are headed by women who earn lower wages than men and are more likely than men to work part time, it can be even more difficult to find sufficient money to pay a mortgage and the outgoings on an owner-occupied home. Banks or Building Societies will lend on a mortgage about $2^1/_2$–3 times your gross annual salary. They will lend generally for a period of up to 25 years, but a shorter period may be required of those who are regarded as a greater risk. Your local council may be able to help you by nominating you to a local building society.

Some single parents may find that their age is used against them, (they are regarded as too old to be able to pay back a mortgage during their working life) or the fact that they work part time may cause problems over the amount the lender will be prepared to lend. Irregular income, such as maintenance payments may also cause the lender to worry about accepting your application.

It may also be difficult to raise enough cash to put down as a deposit during the purchase of the property, at exchange of contracts stage. This is usually 10% of the purchase price. It is possible to ask for a smaller amount to be accepted.

In addition, you are unlikely to get a 100% mortgage unless you are buying a new house, and not always then. So you will need to find the extra capital to make up the purchase price. Other costs to remember are the solicitor's fees, stamp duty if it is payable, and the costs of actually moving in – the removal van, connection of gas, electricity and phone, and paying the insurance on the building, the water rates and service charges if there are any.

2. *Shared Ownership*

In some areas, local authorities and housing associations run shared ownership schemes. This means that you can apply to buy a home in stages. You purchase a proportion of your home on a mortgage and rent the rest on a fair rent from the council or housing association. You can later increase the proportion that you are buying. It may be worth contacting your local authority and local housing association to see if there are any such schemes in your area.

3. *Buying a Council House*

Council and housing association tenants have been given the right to buy their homes at a discount. Obviously you have to be a tenant before you can buy. The amount of discount you will get will depend on how long you have lived there.

If you sell the home within a set period of time, you may have to repay the discount. It is important to remember this if your marriage or relationship breaks down during this time as you may have to repay some money to the council if your home is sold as part of the divorce settlement or court order.

4. *Renting a Home from a Local Authority or Housing Association*

It can be difficult to rent a home from a council or housing association unless you are actually homeless or have a high priority for housing on medical or other grounds. You can apply to be on the local council housing waiting list, but you may have to wait many years before getting a house. If you own your own home you may not be able to go on the waiting list.

Many housing associations only accept people who are nominated by the local council or other local agencies, others allow you to apply to them direct.

5. *Transfers*

Both housing associations and local councils have schemes that allow you to apply to move from your home in one area to one in another area. You should approach your existing landlord – either council or housing association – and explain where you need to move to and why, and ask to be nominated to your chosen area.

In addition, you may be able to arrange a mutual exchange of your home with someone else. You will have to get the permission of your landlord before it can go ahead.

6. *Renting a Home from a Private Landlord*

Rented accommodation is generally scarce and expensive and private landlords are not keen on renting to people with children. The law on private tenancies is very complicated and has been radically changed by the Housing Act 1988, which came into force on 15 January 1989. From that date the majority of new private tenancies will be what are known as assured tenancies and not the protected tenancies of the old legislation. This means that a market rent can be charged and rent regulation is minimal. The tenant is still protected from eviction – a court order is still required – but the grounds for eviction by the court are much wider than under the old law. Protected tenancies created before 1989 are not affected by the new law. If you have this kind of tenancy you may be able to get a fair rent registered on the property instead of having to pay a high rent demanded by the landlord. In addition, you may have the right to stay in the property for as long as you want to. Provided you pay the rent and keep to all the obligations of the tenancy agreement the landlord is unlikely to be able to regain possession of the property.

As the law is now even more complicated than it was, it is vital to get good detailed advice about your rights in relation to any tenancy you may have or are wanting to have.

7. Tied Accommodation

It is possible to get a job where your accommodation is included, e.g. housekeeper, caretaker, or a job where you need to live close to your work. Similarly, the armed forces, police and some public authorities give accommodation to their staff and their families.

There will be problems with your tied home if you leave your job, or if your home was tied to your spouse's job and he or she leaves. In some circumstances you may have to leave your home. Get advice, but do not leave your home unless you are sure that you have to.

B. KEEPING YOUR EXISTING HOME

How can you keep your home, if this is what you want to do, when a relationship breaks down? The law treats married and unmarried couples in a different way so the right to stay in the home or keep it after the end of a relationship depends on whether or not you are or were married. As usual, the law is complicated so get advice before leaving your home or before agreeing to any settlement.

1. Home Owners

What rights do I have to stay in my home?
If you are married then you have the right to stay in your matrimonial home for as long as you remain married.

The Matrimonial Homes Act 1983 gives both spouses the right to live in their matrimonial home, unless a court orders otherwise. If the house is in the name of one spouse only, then the other spouse can protect his or her rights in the home by registering them by way of a notice under the Matrimonial Homes Act 1983. This notice will warn anyone who tries to buy the home or to grant a further loan on it that the spouse who lives there may have rights in relation to that home. So a non-owning spouse should always register his or her right to occupy the home. A solicitor or Citizens' Advice Bureau will tell you how.

Where you both own the home, you both have an equal right to live in it, and it cannot be sold or mortgaged without both of you agreeing. If you cannot agree, the court will have to impose a solution.

Can I evict my spouse?
You may want to live in the home by yourself, especially if your spouse is violent or making family life impossible. If so, you may be able to get an order (often known as an injunction) removing him or her from the home. The court will take all the circumstances into account and, in particular, if a wife is at risk of violence or there has already been violence, then the court may grant an order. Also, if the children are at risk, then the court will take that very seriously. However, if you simply do not want to live together any more, the court is unlikely to make any order preventing your spouse from living in the matrimonial home.

What is the position if we are not married?
If you are not married to your partner then you are not protected by the Matrimonial Homes Act. Your rights to stay in the home will depend on who owns it and whether you have been given any other contractual rights to stay

in the home for a period of time. The law on property for unmarried couples is very complicated and not very satisfactory – particularly for women – so it is very important that you get good advice about your position.

If you are joint owners, both of you have the right to live in the home. You may become a joint owner in a number of ways, e.g. by a formal agreement or by contributing to the purchase price (paying mortgage instalments) over a period of time. If you are not a joint or a sole owner, then you will probably have few rights to stay in the home if your partner tells you to go. For example, if you are simply living in your boy friend's house with his permission and he tells you to go, unless there are special circumstances you will be entitled to stay only for a reasonable period of 'notice' and then you will have to leave. If you had a particular longer-term agreement when you moved in with your partner, then you may be able to get a court to enforce that agreement.

In addition, if your partner has been violent to you or has threatened violence, you may be able to obtain an order preventing him from molesting you and removing him from the home for a period if you want to go back and if it will be safe for you to do so.

What will happen to the home on my divorce?

If you are married and cannot agree who should keep the home, or how it should be divided between you, the court in divorce, judicial separation or nullity proceedings will decide.

The court has wide powers under matrimonial legislation to transfer the home or part of it, or order a sale. It must consider your needs, those of your spouse, your children and any other relevant circumstances, and then try to make a fair division. In any case, where the children of your marriage are under 18 years old the court must give first consideration to their welfare. Obviously the question of where they live is crucial.

Sometimes the court may award the whole of the home to the spouse who is going to look after the children. Another solution is to allow the custodial parent to continue to live in the house while the children are still in full-time education, and then order the home to be sold and the proceeds divided. Alternatively, the court may decide that the home should be sold immediately and the proceeds of sale divided in whatever proportion seems fair.

In considering any settlement or proposal on the home you should bear in mind the following :

(a) Check that you will be able to cope financially with any new arrangements. It is no good agreeing to keep the home if you cannot pay the mortgage and other outgoings.

(b) Check that any short-term settlement will not have any long-term disadvantages. For example, if you agree to the home being sold in the future, will you be able to house yourself at that stage? Do not rely on the local authority to help you with housing.

(c) Check what will happen if your circumstances change. You might want to move to another area because the job or school prospects are better, or to be near relatives or because the home is too big/small/old/expensive to run. Will the proposed settlement allow you to change your circumstances?

(d) Check that legal aid does not cause problems. If you received legal aid in order to sort out disputes over your home, then the Law Society may have the right to recoup the costs of your case from the value of your share of the home. This is known as the statutory charge, and it can reduce the amount of money you receive once the home is sold. It is important to see whether this applies to you.

(e) Check that you are happy with the proposals on

the home or that they are the best you can get in the circumstances. Court orders on the home are generally final orders and you cannot go back later and ask the court for something different just because your life is changed.

Suppose we are not married; what happens to the home if we split up?

If you are not married to your partner and have no legal interest in the home (e.g. your name is not on the title deed or you have not made any financial contribution to its purchase) then, generally, you will have no right to claim a share in it once the relationship ends.

However, where there is any form of joint ownership in the home the court is able to make an order to sell it or divide the proceeds under the ordinary Law of Property Act 1925. Matrimonial legislation does not apply in these circumstances. In making a decision the court will be concerned to give effect to any agreement you have drawn up relating to the home. If there is no agreement, the court will look at the contributions which you each have made to the purchase of the home to calculate your shares. Just because the home is put in sole or joint names does not necessarily mean that the court will decide that the home is equally or solely owned. If you put in money towards the purchase of the home or paid for substantial improvements to it then the court will take that into account.

However, the court will give you a share in the home only if you have made direct or indirect financial con-tributions to it. Where a woman stays at home, does housework and brings up the children, the court does not consider that she has thereby acquired a financial stake in the home. It does not matter how long you have lived together. In one recent case a woman lost everything as 'all' she had done was to stay at home for 20 years, looking after the man the children and the home! The court did not accept that she had made any direct or indirect contribution to the purchase of the home.

2. Private Tenants

What rights do I have to stay in my home?
If you or your partner are private tenants, the first thing to do is to find out what kind of tenancy you have.

Is there anything in writing? In whose name is the tenancy or agreement? Some private tenants have no long-term security in their home, their rights are very limited and the landlord will have the right to get the home back. Much depends on the sort of agreement the tenants signed, when they moved in and whether the landlord lives in the same premises as them. Any advice here can only be quite general and does not deal with all the different sorts of tenancies or letting agreements. It is very important to get more advice before taking any steps, and in particular before beginning any court proceedings or before contacting the landlord.

In practice, you are likely to have the right to stay in the home for a substantial time only if you have a protected or statutory tenancy and the landlord has no grounds for bringing the tenancy agreement to an end. If your tenancy was created after January 1989 you will probably have an assured tenancy and your rights to stay are not so secure as with protected tenancies.

Whatever tenancy you have, you do not have to leave unless you have been given a proper notice to quit and a court has made a possession order.

Can my partner evict me from our rented home?
If you are married and your home is a protected, assured or statutory tenancy, then you have the right to remain in your matrimonial home. It does not matter that the

tenancy is in your spouse's name, or that it is in joint names. It does not matter if the legal tenant has left. Under the Matrimonial Homes Act 1983 a spouse has the right to stay in the matrimonial home, to pay the rent to the landlord and to be treated by the landlord as if he or she is the actual tenant. The landlord cannot turn round and refuse to deal with you if you are married to the tenant, whether or not your spouse is still around.

However, these rights last only for as long as you remain married, and so it is very important to remember that this protection ceases on divorce.

If you are not married then your rights to remain in the home depend both on what sort of tenancy it is, and whether it is in your name or in joint names with your partner. If it is in your partner's name alone, then if he or she tells you to go, you will probably have to go once a reasonable period has been allowed for you to find somewhere else. Do get advice before you go.

If your partner has been violent to you or you have been threatened with violence or your children are at risk, you may be able to ask the court for orders that your partner is not to molest you and must leave the home. These orders are temporary, generally no longer than three months. If you have no long-term right to stay in the home, you will have to consider carefully whether you want to get back into the home for such a relatively short time. It may be that you would rather go to a Women's Aid refuge or, if you are eligible, apply to the local council as homeless.

If you are a sole or joint tenant then you have the right to stay in the home for as long as the tenancy lasts. If you have a joint tenancy and your partner goes, you still have the right to remain on your own.

Can I get the home permanently transferred to me?

If you are married and need to sort out your long-term position, then you can apply in your divorce, judicial separation or nullity proceedings for the court to settle the future of the tenancy. Again, if it is a protected, statutory or assured tenancy, you can ask the court to transfer a joint tenancy into your sole name, or ask for the tenancy in your spouse's sole name to be transferred to you. The court will consider all the circumstances and in particular the welfare of any children of the marriage who are under 18 years of age.

In some circumstances the landlord will be told of the application to change the tenancy but he does not have a right to prevent a transfer. It is very important that you think carefully about your long-term position because the protection given by the Matrimonial Homes Act may be lost on divorce unless you ask the court to extend it. If you do nothing about the home on divorce you could lose any rights you had.

If you are not married, then you have even fewer options ahead of you. If it is not your tenancy and your partner wants you to leave the home then, in the end you will have to go. If it is your tenancy and you want your partner to leave the home, then he or she will have to go after a reasonable period of time.

If it is a joint tenancy and you cannot agree on who should stay in the home, there may be no way you can apply to the court to resolve it. You will have to try to resolve it between you. If it is absolutely intolerable and you have to leave, then you could try your local council for help, but they are unlikely to assist unless you had actually been at risk of violence or there had already been violence, in which case they may have a legal obligation to help you. See the earlier part of this chapter on home-lessness. If you are in this situation you will need expert legal advice.

3. Council and Housing Association Tenants

Most single parents are currently council or housing association tenants, because the private rented sector is too expensive. The individual council or housing association manage the housing, though in the case of council housing some estates may be taken over by private or other landlords when the Housing Act of 1988 comes into force. Some councils have sympathetic policies on relationship breakdown and will try, if necessary, to rehouse both partners, whether or not they are married and whoever has custody of the children. Others are not interested in such a policy and will assist only those they are legally obliged to. It is always worthwhile finding out what your council's policy is. Local councillors and your MP, together with local advice agencies should be able to advise you further.

Can my partner evict me from a council home?

If you are married, you have the right to remain in your council home whether or not the tenancy is in your name. The Matrimonial Homes Act 1983 gives you the right to pay the rent to the council and you can stay even if your spouse (the tenant) has gone. Your rights are no greater than the original tenant but you are treated as having equivalent rights for as long as you remain married.

In addition, if there is violence or a threat of violence or your children are at risk, then you can apply to the court for an order removing your spouse from the home and an order preventing him from molesting you. It is obviously important to make sure that you will be safe if you go back home. Get advice from one of the agencies in Chapter 9. You should not be forced to go back home if you will be at risk of further violence if you do so.

If you are not married, your rights to remain in the home will depend on whether you are the tenant. If you are the sole tenant or a joint tenant, you have the right to remain. If you are not the tenant, and if the tenant tells you to go, you will have to leave once you have been given a reasonable period of time to look for somewhere else. If you are the tenant and you want your partner to leave, then he or she will have to go eventually, after a reasonable period of time has been given for him or her to find somewhere else to live.

If you are joint tenants, you both have the right to remain.

As with married couples, if there is violence or the threat of violence, then you may be able to obtain a court order preventing further violence or removing your partner from the home. You must obviously consider what your rights to the tenancy are and whether you want to stay or to return to the tenancy if you have left.

Can the actual tenancy be transferred to me?

If you are married to your partner you can apply in divorce, judicial separation or nullity proceedings for the court to transfer your tenancy. It is no longer possible for a council or housing association to change the tenancy from one person to another unless you both agree. If you don't agree then only the court can sort it out. The court will take all the circumstances into account and in particular the welfare of any children of the marriage under 18 years of age. The court can change a joint tenancy into a sole tenancy or transfer the tenancy from one person to another, depending on the needs of you, your spouse and children.

If you are not married to your partner then it is not possible to apply to the court to resolve any problem over the tenancy. The court has no power to alter or transfer the tenancy except sometimes if it is a joint tenancy. If you and your partner cannot agree then it is worth seeing whether the council would be prepared to offer one of you a separate tenancy. They do not have to help you unless you have to leave home because of violence and it is not possible for you to return. See the earlier sections in this chapter on homelessness.

If you are the tenant then obviously you have the right to remain. If you are not the tenant then you have no long-term rights in the home. If you are joint tenants then you both have the right to stay.

Can I get help if my home needs repairs?

Getting the home repaired and improved can be an enormous problem for single parents. If you are a tenant, your landlord will have certain obligations to maintain the structure and exterior of your home, and many of the major internal items – like the toilet and water supply. If your landlord fails to carry out the necessary work, you may have the right to go to court. You should contact the local council Environmental Health Department and get advice on whether to take action to enforce your rights. Do not withhold your rent unless you have taken advice. If you do withhold the rent, do save the money, otherwise you may run the risk of your landlord being successful in bringing proceedings to evict you.

If you are an owner-occupier, you may be able to get help from the council towards paying for essential repairs and improvements. There is sometimes a long waiting list for grants. A grant will not meet the entire cost and will depend on your exact circumstances.

If you are on income support you may be able to get a loan to cover essential repairs and maintenance. It must be emphasized that this is a loan and will be repaid by deductions from your income support payments.

2: Legal Care and Custody of the Children

The law in this area is recognized as being in a complete mess. Different pieces of legislation use different terms to mean the same thing and rights in relation to children are complex and confusing. It is even worse if you are not married to the other parent or you are not the child's natural parent. A new bill, the Children Bill, which will simplify everything considerably is currently being considered by Parliament. However it is unlikely to become law until the autumn of 1990 at the earliest. What is described here is the current situation, with some indications of what changes are likely to take place in the future.

This chapter deals with the position for married and unmarried parents and their children and also for those who care for children who are not their own.

As the law is difficult and the future of children so important, it is essential that you get good detailed advice if you are at all worried. Good legal advice at the outset can prevent costly and damaging court cases which harm everyone, including, of course, the children.

Remember that this deals with the law in England and Wales. If your marriage took place abroad, or your spouse is living abroad and has close links with that country then the laws of that country may affect your child.

A. MARRIED PARENTS

What rights do I have in relation to my child?
Parents who are married to each other have equal rights and duties towards their children. Neither parent is

superior to the other and the days when wives had no legal rights over their children are long gone.

In recent years there has been a move away from looking at 'rights' and more emphasis has been put on the duties and responsibilities of parenthood. These change and diminish as your child grows older and is able to exercise independent choices about the future. (Under the new law this will be even more marked. The new Bill will replace the notion of parental rights with a new concept of parental responsibilities, which both married parents will have in respect of their children. The notion of 'rights' will be abolished.)

Obviously, while your child is young you have a duty to care for and protect your child, and have the responsibility to make sure that your child is developing and thriving in a proper way. A child must receive education suitable to his or her needs between the ages of 5 years and 16 years. The Education Authority has the obligation to provide the schooling; the parents have the obligation to see that the child goes to school. You can decide to educate your child yourself, but the local education authority will want to check that the education you are providing is adequate. If they do not think it is, they can take you to court to insist that your child is given a different education.

If it is believed that a child is in danger, or is being abused or ill-treated, the local authority Social Services Department or even the police can intervene and take the parents to court to decide whether the child should be removed from home.

Subject to this, parents have a relatively free hand to decide themselves how to bring up a child, which is fine as long as you are able to agree.

If you separate or get divorced, your legal situation in relation to your children does not automatically change. Both of you can continue to retain all rights and responsibilities in relation to your children if that is what you wish, though, obviously, if you are not living together any more then the children will generally live with one parent most of the time.

On divorce, the court must consider the arrangements for the children and say whether those arrangements are satisfactory. One or both parents will have to attend a court hearing, generally referred to as the 'children's appointment'. This is a short hearing and is regarded by lawyers as being a formality where there is no dispute between the parents.

If you are not getting divorced, you do not have to go to court or obtain any order but you may wish to do so.

What does a custody order mean?
Either spouse can apply for a custody order giving him or her sole custody of a child.

An application can be made in the context of matrimonial proceedings, but you do not have to start matrimonial proceedings in order to ask for a custody order. Proceedings can be brought separately in the magistrates' court under the Domestic Proceedings and Magistrates Courts Act 1978, or under the Guardianship of Minors Act 1971 & 1973 in the magistrates', County or High courts. In addition, custody can be awarded by the High Court in wardship proceedings. This is an example of the current confusion of proceedings that can be used.

A sole custody order will normally give you the right to have the child live with you and to make all the important decisions about your child's life. The other parent may be granted a right of access (see below).

Sometimes parents are told that they need a custody order in order to qualify for housing, or even before a school will show a parent the child's school reports. This is not true and it is important that you do not get pushed into going to court at great expense simply for someone

else's administrative convenience. You should only go to
court because you want or need to go yourself.

What is a joint custody order?
In divorce proceedings the court can also grant joint
custody. This does not mean that the child has to live with
both of you but that you both retain responsibilities and
rights over your child. Obviously, the court must also
decide when making the order which parent the child is
actually going to live with. In the event of a dispute that
you cannot resolve, the matter would have to go back to
court.

Although joint custody orders are very popular in some
areas of the country, it is important to consider whether
in fact it would be a good idea for you. Joint custody is a
workable solution if you and your spouse can agree about
the children and are on good enough terms to be able to
resolve any difficulties. You do not want an order that is
simply going to involve continual aggravation between
you and involve return trips to court to sort out the difficulties. The advantage of joint custody is that it allows the
parent with whom the child does not live to feel that he or
she has a stake in their child's life, and is not just someone
who comes to visit occasionally. Both parents still have
the right to be involved in decisions about the child's
upbringing, such as education, medical treatment,
religion and so on. But it is not desirable for any parent to
be coerced into accepting joint custody if it is not in fact
the best solution in the circumstances.

What is care and control?
Care and control is given to the parent with whom the
child is going to live. The order allows that parent to
make all the sorts of choices necessary when caring for
the child on a regular basis. Major decisions will be made
by the parent who has custody or by the parents jointly.

It is not considered a good idea to give care and control to one parent without also giving that parent custody. Obviously if you are looking after your child on a regular basis you are also likely to want to be involved in the major decisions in that child's life. (Under the new Bill this will be replaced by a simpler order known as a residence order which will simply state with whom a child is to live.)

What is access?

Access means visiting or otherwise contacting children. It can range from the odd visit once or twice a year to regular meetings several times a week or staying with a person for weekends and holidays. Although many access orders are made by the court, research has shown that nearly two-thirds of them have completely broken down or are non-existent after a few years. Many children lose touch with their fathers as it is generally fathers who are concerned to get access and mothers who get care and control. Problems often arise if either parent moves to a new area. Sometimes one or other parent finds it too difficult to visit or just loses interest.

If you are in agreement with your spouse about access to the children, you don't have to get an order specifying what access should be awarded – the order might simply state 'reasonable access' and it will be left up to you to work out what arrangements suit you all.

If there is likely to be friction about access, then it is better to specify conditions in the order, e.g. access once a week on Wednesdays and staying access for alternate weekends. If you don't want your partner to come to your home to pick up the children, then it might be possible for grandparents, friends or even a social worker to help with this.

The court is generally reluctant to refuse access altogether, but can do so if it is in the child's best interests.

How does the court make a decision on custody or access?

The court must put the child's welfare as its first and paramount consideration. This means that in the end it is what the court thinks is best for the child that will carry most weight.

Most cases are settled by agreement and the court will simply accept this without much investigation. However, if there is a dispute it is quite likely that the court will order a welfare report to be prepared. A probation officer or social worker will interview the parents, children and everyone else who is important to the child, such as grandparents or teachers, in order to prepare a report for the court.

The court and the welfare officer will want to know about where your child is living at the moment, what changes are proposed, the age and whereabouts of any brothers or sisters and proposals for them. The court will also take into account your child's age, emotional and educational needs, and any physical or mental handicap your child may have.

In addition the court will want to know what your child wants. Your child's views will obviously be more important the older he or she is. In the end the court will decide what it thinks is best for your child, which will not necessarily be what your child wants.

What decision is the most likely on custody and access?

In most cases the court continues the 'status quo'. That is, the parent who is looking after the child up to the date of the court hearing continues to do so. So, if you want custody, try to keep your children with you. Don't leave them behind in the home unless you are absolutely certain that there is no alternative.

If your child is still under five years old then it is likely that custody will go to the mother, as courts tend to feel that young children need their mother.

Courts do not like splitting up brothers and sisters unless it is absolutely necessary.

Your 'matrimonial' behaviour generally should not be relevant to the question of custody of your children, unless it could be harmful to them. If you take drugs or abuse alcohol, custody may be denied, as it may if you have a history of mental illness. Some unconventional lifestyles are not favourably regarded by courts. If you follow a strict religious belief which involves isolating the children from ordinary life, the courts will be concerned. Gay or lesbian parents may face difficulties. In the past it has proved extremely difficult for lesbian women to keep custody of their children even though there has been no evidence to show that they are not able to care for them.

What is conciliation and can it help?

Conciliation services are voluntary organizations which differ widely. They have been set up to assist parents who are experiencing difficulties in custody and access disputes and try to help them reach agreement rather than go to court. They take the view that parents are the best people to sort these problems out and that going to court is generally pretty unsatisfactory for everyone concerned. Conciliators see people at different stages of the proceedings. Some get involved even before any court proceedings have been commenced. Others accept referrals once a divorce petition has been filed or once an application for custody or access is going to be contested. Others will deal with existing orders which are not working out properly.

Some schemes are completely independent of the court; some are part of the court although they operate as a separate unit. Some work as part of the civil work team attached to the court welfare service. It is in no way compulsory to use these schemes, and if you do not feel they are helping don't feel obliged to continue.

The local Citizen's Advice Bureau or the court will know whether there is a conciliation service local to you, and what sort of scheme it is.

Can my child be taken into care on divorce?

In divorce, judicial separation and nullity proceedings, if the court is satisfied that there are 'exceptional circumstances' and that no other course is possible it can order that your child does not remain with either of you, but is placed in the care of the local authority. In addition, the court can make a supervision order which allows a social worker to supervise your child at home.

Can I adopt my child with my new partner?

If you divorce and then remarry it is not uncommon for your new spouse to want to adopt your child. This is possible, but the court will not like the idea in general as it cuts off the other natural parent from all links with the child. The court will probably consider that a joint custody order in favour of you and your new spouse is adequate. The court might be prepared to allow an adoption if the child wants it and the other parent is not at all involved. Unmarried couples cannot adopt a child jointly, even where one of them is the child's natural parent.

My husband is my child's stepfather; can he claim custody or access?

Yes he can. He does not automatically acquire any parental rights or duties in relation to your children simply by having married you. However, after he has lived with you and your children as a family, he does have a right, on divorce or separation, to apply for custody or access to the children. He must show that he treated the children as children of the family, i.e. that he has accepted responsibility for them himself. Some stepfathers may have behaved as though they were a natural father to the children for years and will naturally wish to maintain links. Equally the child may want this. The court will decide this question as with all questions relating to children – what is in the child's best interests?

Can anyone other than a parent or stepparent claim custody of the children?

In theory, it is possible, on divorce, for the court to award custody to a third party, e.g. a relative or friend. This rarely happens and the court will only do so if it is clearly in the child's best interests. But if your mother or sister, for instance, has looked after your child for a substantial period and there was some good reason why you should not have custody, then it could be granted to one of them.

B. UNMARRIED PARENTS

The law is changing on unmarried parents in relation to their children. A Family Law Reform Act was passed in 1987 to do this but has not yet been brought fully into force. Moreover, further changes will take place once the Children Bill of 1989 is brought into force (not likely before autumn 1990). So there are going to be changes, probably soon after this book is published. It will be necessary to check the position with an adviser before relying on the law as it is stated here. Described below is the existing law and the likely changes to it, where that is appropriate.

Obviously the law has to deal with different situations. Some unmarried couples live together and bring up children together. But often the mother alone brings up the child and the father is not involved. Some fathers retain a lively interest in the child but do not live with the child or the mother. The new legislation has tried to deal with all types of situations by allowing the father greater opportunities to apply to the court to obtain rights in relation to his child, but by retaining the mother's automatic rights over her child to give her that much needed security.

Who has the right to custody of a non-marital child?

Unlike married parents, unmarried parents do not start off by having equal rights over their children. Only the mother has automatic parental rights. She does not need to apply to the court for a custody order because she has custody by virtue of being the mother.

It is not currently possible to share legal custody or get a joint custody order between unmarried parents, even if they agree or live together. (This will change when the Children Bill 1989 becomes law.)

A father can make an application for custody to the court under the Guardianship of Minors Act 1971. The court must decide on the basis of the child's best interests and can grant custody to the father instead of the mother. The court cannot grant a joint custody order. Under the Family Law Reform Act 1987, however, both parents will be able to apply to the court to share parental rights. It also allows unmarried couples to draw up a legal agreement sharing rights over their children. Once again, the court would always have the right to overrule any agreement if it was not in the child's best interests. These changes came into force in the Spring of 1989.

Once the father has been granted custody (or has shared parental rights under the new law), he can, as can the mother, appoint a guardian for the child in his will. He will also be allowed to include the child on his passport.

Can a father apply for access to a non-marital child?

Yes. The father has the right to apply to the court for access to his child if no agreement on this can be reached. The court will generally allow access, particularly if the father has played any part in the child's life up until now. Even in cases where the father has never been involved, for example where the relationship broke up as soon as the mother knew she was pregnant, the court will still generally take the view that it is good for the child to have contact with both parents if at all possible.

The court can order that access should be supervised by a social worker or probation officer if there are problems. If it is considered to be against the child's best interests then access can be terminated by the court.

How do you prove who is the father?

Whenever there is an application to the court in relation to a non-marital child there may be a dispute as to who is the father. This the court must decide. It must be proved 'on a balance of probabilities' and generally requires cogent evidence. One method is to do blood tests on the parents and the child which will show that a person with a particular blood group could not be the father. The court can order these tests, but it cannot force you to give blood if you object. If you do object, the court is likely to infer that whatever you are saying about paternity is not true. So a mother who alleges that a particular man is the father of her child but who refuses a blood test will not win her case. New testing techniques called 'DNA finger-printing' have recently been introduced here, and these are considered to be 100% accurate. They are much more accurate than blood tests and can also be ordered by the court to establish paternity.

The Family Law Reform Act 1987 will introduce a new right for the child to apply for declaration of parentage. If the child is too young to bring legal proceedings on his or her own, then a parent or guardian can act on the child's behalf.

Can I adopt my own non-marital child?
Sometimes single mothers wanted to apply to adopt their own children so that the child became the 'legitimate' child of the mother and loses all links with the father. A single mother and her new husband might also apply to adopt jointly. Even a single father might apply to adopt (provided he was actually looking after the child).

The courts, are, however, not very keen to make such adoption orders unless the other parent is dead or cannot be found. The court tends to feel that links with a natural parent should be preserved if possible, especially if he or she has contact with the child. The consent of the mother is normally needed for an adoption. The father's consent is not needed unless he has custody, but the court will not make an adoption order without seeking his views if he is available.

C. ALL PARENTS

Can an order for custody or access be changed?
Where a child is concerned, no order in relation to custody, access, parental rights, etc. is ever final. It is always open to the parents, whether they are married or not, to go back to the court to vary the order if the circumstances have changed or the order is no longer suitable. But no court likes constant applications where there are no grounds. It is much better to try to make the order work – or to come to some agreement if adjustments have to be made.

How can access orders be enforced?
Court orders are not always obeyed, especially access

orders. Sometimes the child refuses to see the 'access' parent. Sometimes it is the custodial parent who has prejudiced the child against the other parent or is preventing access. If you try to prevent access in breach of a court order you are in contempt of court, and you could be fined or imprisoned. However, imprisonment is unlikely – as is a fine – because it would not be in the child's best interests. There are other risks in defying court orders, besides imprisonment. The court is not likely to trust you again if you subsequently want its help. If you refuse access in a way that causes distress to the children, the court might look again at the original order. It might conclude that the children should not be living with you after all. Some mothers resent the fact that a father is insisting on his access whilst, at the same time, failing to pay maintenance that he has been ordered to pay. The courts will not, however, use access as a means of punishing a father for maintenance default. Nor will it relieve a father of the duty to maintain because a mother is denying access.

What if my partner takes our child abroad and won't return him or her?

'Kidnapping' is a difficult problem to deal with. If you fear it might happen, then you need to get a court order as soon as possible to prevent it. This is often done most speedily by making the child a ward of court. Then the court will order that all ports and airports should watch out to prevent the child from being taken out of the country. You will need legal advice speedily.

If you have a custody order and your child has actually been taken abroad and not returned, then you may be able to start procedures to get the child returned under the Child Abduction and Custody Act 1985. You can get legal aid to pay for a solicitor for this and you should act swiftly, as delay prejudices the chances of success.

D. LOCAL AUTHORITIES AND CARE OF CHILDREN

The children of single parents are among the largest group of those children who go into local authority care at some time or another. This is partly because of the pressure of bringing up a child on your own and partly as a result of the fact that single parents are often poor and live in bad housing. In addition, there may be no one else to care for the child if, for example, you have to go into hospital. Some social workers expect single parents to be less likely to be able to cope with their own children, and instead of assisting with the practical problems of poverty, etc. may concentrate on the fact of single parent-hood itself. Do resist any attempt to treat you like a lesser being just because you are a single parent! There is plenty of evidence to show that single parents are just as good parents as anyone else. Remind the social worker of that fact if necessary. Do not agree to your child going into care or staying in care unless you are sure it is the right decision.

The law on child care will be radically altered once the Children Bill 1989 becomes law. This will probably be sometime in 1990. See the forthcoming *Children's Rights Handbook* in this series.

What will happen if I ask the local authority for help?

The authority should first seek to do all it can to prevent your children coming into care by providing help in cash or kind. However it may be that the right solution to your particular difficulty is to allow the authority to receive your child into voluntary care for a temporary period, such as when you are ill, or when the stress of caring for a child on your own may just prove too much at a par-ticular time. Temporary care can give you time to cope with your problems and the social workers should help you. It is important that you keep in contact with your child during this time if that is possible, otherwise you will risk losing him or her.

As your child will be in voluntary care you have the right to ask for your child back home whenever you wish. However, if he or she has been in voluntary care for more than 6 months then you have to give the social workers 28 days' notice of your wish to have your child back. If the local authority takes the view that you should not have your child back, they may take steps to make the voluntary care more permanent. This is done at the present time by passing a parental rights resolution (see below) or by making the child a ward of court. In such a case you will need to contact a solicitor urgently. The longer children are settled with substitute parents, the harder it is to get them back.

How can the local authority prevent the return of my child?

If your child is in voluntary care (see above) the local authority may pass a 'parental rights resolution'. The effect of this is that the local authority takes over all parental rights and you are not able to ask for your child back. You will get a notice telling you that the resolution has been passed. You then have the right to object to this within 28 days of receiving the notice. If you do object, the matter has to go to the juvenile court within 14 days and the magistrates will decide whether your child should remain in care or whether he or she should go home with you. It is very important that you get good advice, and if you are given any forms that you do not understand take them to an advice centre or solicitor immediately.

If the case is referred to court, you should be entitled to legal aid to help present your case. The Law Society now keeps lists of solicitors who are particularly trained in child-care law cases.

41

The court might decide to appoint a solicitor to represent your child in court separately from yourself.

There is a code of guidance which tells local authorities how to use parental rights resolutions. These resolutions are to be abolished under the Children Bill 1989, which is not yet in force. Under this Act if a local authority thinks a child should be in its care it will have to go to the court from the very beginning and seek to prove its case.

Can my child be taken into care without my consent or a court order?

Yes, this can be done under what are known as place of safety orders. These apply in emergencies where the police or social worker think that a child may be at risk of harm. A police officer or social worker can apply to a single magistrate (at court or at home, during the day or the night) for a place of safety order if they can show that they reasonably fear for the safety of your child. They are then authorized to take your child away from home to a safe place. You should be told of the order as soon as possible after it is granted. The order lasts for up to 28 days (8 days for orders obtained by the police), but are often made for a shorter period. During that time you do not have the right to see your child nor is there any way of challenging the order. However, you should ask the social workers to allow you to visit or to telephone or write to your child.

The local authority must go to court if it wants to keep your child after the place of safety order expires. If the local authority does this then it is up to the court to decide whether there are grounds for making a care order. If the authority does not go to court, you are entitled to the return of your child when the place of safety order expires.

These orders will change considerably when the Children Bill 1989 becomes law. Then there will be what will be called emergency protection orders and these will be granted only by a court. They will last for only 8 days and a parent will be able to go to court to challenge them after 3 days. The court will be able to make directions about contact with parents or other persons and about the medical examination of children. At the time of going to press, these provisions are not yet in force.

What is a care order and when will one be made?

Under the Children and Young Persons Act 1969 the local authority can bring your child before a Juvenile Court if it believes that the child is not developing properly or is at risk of harm in some way. This action may follow a place of safety order or you may receive a summons requiring you to attend court.

You will need legal representation if this happens, and you will probably be entitled to legal aid.

The local authority will have to prove that the facts that it alleges about your child are correct and that your child needs to be in care. If the case is proved, the court can make a care order. This gives the local authority all parental rights, i.e. the right to make all the major decisions about your child, including where your child shall live and how often you shall see him or her. If the local authority refuses to let you see your child, you can apply to the magistrates' court for an access order. You cannot challenge any other decisions made by the local authority in the court.

The care order can last until the child is 18 years old, but it is possible to apply for it to be revoked before then if circumstances change.

The court could make a supervision order instead of a care order. This means that the child would come home with you but that a social worker has the right to visit you and see your child whenever necessary. A supervision order can last up to three years.

What is wardship?

Instead of going to the magistrates' court and asking for a care order under the Children and Young Persons Act 1969, the local authority can apply to the High Court in wardship proceedings if it thinks that the child is at risk and for some reason the powers in the other courts are insufficient to deal with this particular case. Once a child is a ward of court all major decisions about his or her welfare and upbringing have to be taken by the court.

It is difficult for you as a parent to apply to make a child a ward of court if the child is already in care under a care order or a parental rights resolution.

The court has the right to make all the decisions about the child's life until 18 years of age, but will give the right to care for the child to whoever is appropriate – often the local authority.

You can be represented in the court case and the child may be separately represented.

Once your child is in the care of the local authority, any decision about who the child shall see is up to the authority.

If the local authority refuses to allow you to see your child at all, then you have the right to apply to the court for an access order. However, it is not possible at the moment to apply to the court for an access order if the local authority simply reduces the amount of access rather than terminates it altogether. This will change when the Children Bill 1989 comes into force.

If you wish to complain about access to your child in care, the local authority should provide a complaints system for you to use.

3: Protection Against Violence and Discrimination

Single mothers and their children are often physically abused by their partners and may face a continuing risk of abuse even after separation. How can the law help? There are a number of possibilities which are dealt with in this chapter (and some have also been noted in Chapter 1 on Housing) but it is often difficult to get effective protection. The law cannot prevent violence any more than it can prevent crime. Sometimes the police or the courts are unsympathetic, but there is nowadays a greater realization of the extent and seriousness of these problems than there was a few years ago.

Are criminal proceedings likely to help?

If you have been attacked or threatened by a man with whom you are or have been living, then this is the crime of assault – just as if anyone else had attacked you. The police can intervene and arrest the man and charge him with an offence, either common assault or a more serious offence such as assault occasioning grievous bodily harm or attempted murder. However, the police are often reluctant to intervene in what they describe as 'family or domestic' disputes. This does not mean that the police will not take action in an individual case, and an incident should always be reported to them. They should attend the scene of the incident, and come to your home if you are able to call them. If the man is still there, they might decide to take him away or, if you say you want to leave the home, they should help you to get away.

The police can prosecute the man, and if they do they will obviously require you to give evidence. If they do not prosecute, you can go to the magistrates' court yourself to take out a private summons against the man.

This means you are instituting criminal proceedings against him. You will be prosecuting the case in court, although the police might assist you. This course is not really advisable. You are not entitled to legal aid. On the other hand, the man may be entitled to legal aid as he is being prosecuted. Even if he is convicted, this may not protect you if he is simply bound over to keep the peace, fined or imprisoned for a brief period. Whether you or the police prosecute, you will be obliged to give evidence of the assault.

Can I get a court order that will protect me?

Yes, you can go to a civil court for an injunction to protect you against molestation or to prevent your partner from living in the home. First you must be quite sure that you want the order. Sometimes women are effectively forced to get these injunctions by housing officers. They will sometimes say that they will not accept you as being homeless because of domestic violence unless you have an injunction to prove it. This should not be necessary. All you should be required to do is prove your case to the official, e.g. by a doctor's note or evidence from a neighbour, relative, the police or a social worker. Your solicitor, if you have one, will be able to help with negotiations with the council on this. If you do decide that you need a court order, then what you can do depends on whether or not you are married to your violent partner.

If you are married, there are more ways of getting an order – in the magistrates' court or as part of separation or divorce proceedings, or as part of custody proceedings or directly under the Domestic Violence and Matrimonial Proceedings Act or the Matrimonial Homes Act. If you are not married you can still get an order but you have to use the County court only, under the Domestic Violence and Matrimonial Proceedings Act.

What sort of order can I get?

You can get two types of order. First, a non-molestation order which orders the man not to 'assault, molest or in any way interfere with you'. It can tell him not to do specific things, like contact you at work, phone you or follow you from your home.

The order may have a definite time limit or, more commonly, it may say that it will last 'until further order'. This means that it will last until either you or he applies to change or terminate the order. In the magistrates' court this order is called a personal protection order but it fulfills the same function.

Second, the court may make an ouster or exclusion order. This is an order that removes the man from the home and prevents him from returning to it. It will allow you to return home to live there without him. Such an order will generally have a time limit. It will last for 3 months or else it will be made to last until the other matrimonial proceedings have been finally dealt with. When the order comes to an end it is possible to apply for a further order but there is no guarantee that you will get one.

The court can grant the order whether or not you own or rent the home. The order does not interfere with property rights but is only intended to be a short-term form of protection from violence.

Suppose he won't obey the order?

It is possible to ask the court to add a power of arrest to your order if the man has caused you actual physical harm and is likely to do so again. This power will last up to 3 months. It means that a copy of the court order is filed at your local police station and then the police can arrest him if he breaches the court order. It does not mean that the police must arrest him, merely that they can do so.

This power of arrest can be attached to an order from both the County and the magistrates' courts. It is also possible for the court to fine the man for breach of the order, or to commit him to prison for a period. If the police arrest him under a power of arrest they will bring him to court and a committal to prison for contempt is likely in these circumstances.

How quickly can an order be obtained?

It is possible to apply to a court in an emergency without having to wait for all the papers to be completed or served on the man. This is known as an ex-parte application. You will need a solicitor to help you, and in these particular circumstances emergency legal aid will generally be available. This may cause some delay in getting to court. In exceptional cases it is possible to obtain legal aid the same day and therefore go to court straight away, but it is more common for it to take several days before the solicitor receives the legal aid certificate. Until the legal aid certificate is granted the solicitor will not get paid for going to court.

So, although you can apply to the court without waiting, in practice it may not be possible.

Another reason why your solicitor may advise against going to court straight away for an 'ex-parte' application, is that you are likely to be granted a non-molestation order only. Exclusion orders are not granted ex-parte, so it may be better to wait a few days so that the man can be served with the court papers and then you can apply for both a non-molestation order and an ouster order.

If you are not going to be safe going back home even with the two court injunctions, then there may be little point in asking for them. The court will not grant you an ouster order if you do not intend to return home.

What other ways are there to escape from violence?

Perhaps the best place to start if you are suffering violence or if you are in fear of violence is your local women's refuge. The women involved with the refuge understand exactly what you are experiencing and will be able to give you a lot of practical and emotional support.

It may be necessary for you to stay somewhere temporarily, even if you are going to try to go back home. You may be able to stay in the refuge, or if they are full they will try and find another refuge that could take you. They will know of good local solicitors who are used to dealing with this area of law and they will also know the attitude of your local council.

In some parts of the country, refuges have started up specially for Asian women or black women where they will get support and help from other black or Asian women.

If you do not want to go to a women's refuge, or for some reason they cannot help, it is important to remember that the local council will probably be under a duty to provide at least temporary accommodation if there has been violence or a threat of violence as has been explained in Chapter 1.

What can be done if there is violence to the children?

The court can grant injunctions to protect children in just the same way as it can act to protect women against violence. In addition, the local authority's Social Services Department and the police have powers to act to protect children if they think they are at risk, for example by placing them in a place of safety (see page 42).

If you fear that your child has been or might be kidnapped, then there are several steps that can be taken to try and protect or reclaim the child (see page 39).

My children and I are being racially abused by a neighbour. What can I do?

This type of harassment is likely to amount to a criminal offence. You should report it to the police. It is probably a good idea to seek local help first, or take a friend or relative with you for some support.

You should also report it to the local council. If you are a council tenant they may be prepared to give you priority for a transfer because of what has happened. Some councils have written policies setting out how to deal with this problem. It is worth finding out whether your council will help.

Some councils and also some housing associations have a clause in the tenancy agreement which gives them the right to take action against a tenant who is found to have been violent to another occupier or has harassed them. Even if the tenancy agreement does not contain such a clause, the council may still be able to take action against the tenant who is harassing you, by arguing that they have been a 'nuisance'. This is a difficult area of law and you will need legal advice.

4: Nationality and Immigration

This area of law is one of the most complicated and can also be most important for some single parents as it affects their right to live and work in this country, to return here, and to pass on nationality to their children.

Failure to take the right action, or ignoring time limits can be fatal to your chances, so it is very important that you get good advice. Nationality law changed in this country in 1983, and important changes were made in the rights of children to inherit British citizenship.

This chapter can give only a brief outline of the law. If you are in any doubt, seek advice before you contact the Home Office or the Immigration Authorities about your situation.

My child was born in Britain. Will he be a British citizen?

Until 1 January 1983 if you were born here you were a British citizen. It did not matter whether your parents were British, to be British you only had to be born in this country.

The British Nationality Act 1981 changed this. The rules now are that you become a British Citizen if:

(a) *for legitimate children*: either your mother or your father is a British citizen or is settled here;

(b) *for non-marital children*: your mother is a British citizen or settled here

'Settled' means having lived here by right for at least 5 years without any conditions having been imposed on that right.

My child was born abroad. Can he be a British citizen?

Your child will be a British citizen if born abroad if:

(a) *for legitimate children*: either parent is a British citizen;

(b) *for non-marital children*: the mother is a British citizen.

But the child must be the first generation to be born abroad.

Example: Sarah was born in France to British parents. She is British. She is unmarried and becomes pregnant. Her child Sam, is born in France. Sam will not be a British citizen because he is the second generation to be born abroad.

However, there are provisions which allow children born abroad to British parents who themselves were born abroad to register as British citizens in certain circumstances.

It is important to note that if your parents are not married to each other then you can inherit British citizenship only from your mother. If your mother is not a British citizen or settled here then you cannot become a British citizen but you might be able to inherit your mother's own nationality if her country's laws allow this.

What happens if, as a result of these rules, my child is stateless?

There are special rules to deal with children who are 'stateless' but it may be very difficult to fit into them. A non-marital child with a foreign mother and a British father may be able to persuade the Home Office to register him or her as a British citizen. There is no right to this, although there has been a campaign to allow unmarried fathers to pass on their British nationality to their children.

Can adoption change a child's nationality?

If you are a British citizen and you adopt a child in this country then that child will automatically become a British citizen. If you adopt a child abroad your child will not have the same rights.

Can the marriage of its parents change a child's nationality?

If you marry your child's father at any time after the birth of the child, then your child will be able to inherit British citizenship from either you or your spouse if you are British citizens or settled here.

Do only British citizens have an automatic right to live in this country?

The British Nationality Act 1981 created new categories of British status. Only British citizens have full rights here. Citizens of British Dependent Territories and British Overseas Citizens have limited rights. In particular they do not have the right to live here.

When is it possible to register as a British citizen?

You can apply to the Home Office by completing a form and paying a fee.

Your right to register as a British citizen will depend on your existing status. For example, Commonwealth citizens who have lived in the United Kingdom since 1973 have the right to register. Some former Commonwealth citizens lost their British citizenship when their country of origin became independent. It is important to get advice as some of the provisions on entitlement to register changed from 1 January 1988.

What is naturalization?

Naturalization is not the same as registration as a British citizen as there is no right to naturalization. Naturalization is the process whereby a person who is not a British citizen and has no right to register as one applies to become a British citizen by naturalization. It is up to the Government whether they accept an application or not. Generally to be successful you must have lived here for a set period of time (five years, or three years if you are married to a British citizen). You must have been free from any restrictions imposed upon you when you came here, be of good character, speak or understand English, Welsh or Gaelic and want to make your home here. You have to pay a fee and complete an application form.

Can I or my children have two nationalities at the same time?

Yes, you can be both a British citizen and a citizen of another country. However, some countries make you choose one citizenship only when you become an adult. If you decide to become a British citizen it might affect your right to remain a citizen of another country. For example, Trinidad and India do not allow their citizens to hold dual citizenship.

I am a citizen of an EEC country; can I live in the UK?

Britain's entry into the European Economic Community had an impact on the rights of travel, work and movement for British citizens in the EEC and EEC citizens in this country. EEC countries are Britain, France, West Germany, Belgium, Italy, Spain, Holland, Portugal, Ireland, Greece, Luxembourg and Denmark. EEC citizens are guaranteed free movement within the member states. This means that if you are an EEC citizen you can come to this country without any restriction on your right to work here. You will normally be admitted for a period of 6 months. You are entitled to travel with your family or to be joined by them later.

After 6 months, if you have obtained employment, you should be issued with a residence permit, which normally lasts for 5 years. Residence permits are not issued to the unemployed or persons claiming State benefits.

Can I live in the UK if I am not a British or EEC citizen?

You will be able to come and live in the UK only if you have permission before you leave the country where you have been living. This is called entry clearance, and may be a visa, a letter giving consent for you to come here, or an entry certificate. If you do not have this permission then you will not be allowed in. You must get entry clearance even if you are engaged to or get married to a British citizen. You will then have to live here for 12 months after which time you can apply for settlement here.

The Immigration Officers might also ask a friend or relative in this country to sponsor a person wanting to come here. If you are asked to do this it means that you give an undertaking that you will support that person and give them somewhere to live if necessary.

My children live abroad; can they come and join me here?

If your children are under eighteen and not British citizens they will normally be allowed to join you here for twelve months. After twelve months you can apply for their settlement here. Children who become eighteen during this time can still apply.

In order to get your children here you will have to show that you have sole responsibility for caring for them. Even if you have been sending money abroad regularly to support your child, the Home Office may try to argue that the people who have been looking after your child for you have accepted responsibility for your child.

It is also important not to claim state benefits during

the 12 months that your child is allowed to join you (see below).

What happens if I and my spouse or fiancé split up after I have come here?

If you came here with a spouse or fiancé and you split up within the first year of being here, then you may lose the right to stay here. After one year you can apply for an indefinite right to stay here. If you split up after that is granted then you may be all right.

If your husband is ordered to leave the country or has only restricted rights to stay here then you may have difficulties persuading the Immigration Authorities to let you stay. Do get advice immediately if this happens.

Can I claim State benefits if I am not a British citizen?

Whether or not you are entitled to claim State benefits depends on your immigration status. It is important not to claim these benefits if you are unsure of your immigration or residence rights.

The general principle is that on entry to this Country you must be able to support yourself during your time here and not become a burden on public funds. Claiming a variety of benefits is risky as it may put your right to remain here in jeopardy. In some circumstances you are simply not entitled to any help or financial assistance. 'Public Funds' means the following benefits: income support, housing benefit, family credit, and help from the local authority as a homeless person. Do not make a claim on any public funds without seeking advice.

The following benefits are not public funds: unemployment benefit, invalidity benefit, child benefit, or student grants and you can claim these without endangering your right to remain in this country.

Can I claim treatment from the National Health Service?

Residents are entitled to free treatment from the NHS. Non-residents will be charged. You will be regarded as being a resident if you have lived here for 6 months or more and can convince the NHS of this. You are exempt from charge if you have been here for a year, as is your spouse and any children under sixteen or, if in full-time education, under nineteen years.

You should not have to pay if you live here permanently, or if you are here to work.

5: Money

Poverty is the biggest problem facing single parents. Many are trying to bring up children on an inadequate mixture of State benefits, low wages and private maintenance.

This chapter covers the various forms of State welfare benefits available to single parents and also covers the tax system in outline.

It also looks at the steps a pregnant woman may need to take to claim financial assistance for herself and her child.

A. TAX

It is vital to ensure that you are paying the correct tax and are getting the correct allowances to set against any taxable income. There are particular tax considerations for widows which will be dealt with in this section.

The main principle of the taxation system to remember is that if you are single or living as a single person, then you should be treated as such by the Inland Revenue. Your husband's or partner's income is irrelevant in relation to your tax liability. A married couple living together is dealt with as one unit with the man being entitled to claim an additional married man's allowance. It is quite a complicated system, and it is generally up to you to claim an allowance, so many single parents have missed out over the years. Some Inland Revenue staff can be quite helpful in dealing with problems but you cannot guarantee it.

The figures given below are for the year 1989–90.

What tax allowances can I claim?

The tax you have to pay is worked out by calculating all the income you received during the tax year, which is from the 6 April to the following 5 April, and deducting any allowances you are entitled to. As a single parent, you are entitled to claim two allowances: the single person's tax allowance (currently £2785) and the additional personal allowance (currently £1590). The combination of these two allowances is the same as the married man's tax allowance.

The additional personal allowance can be claimed if you have a child living with you for all or part of the tax year. It stops at the end of the tax year when your youngest child leaves full-time education. You can claim the additional personal allowance even if your ex spouse is still claiming the married man's tax allowance or is paying you maintenance for yourself or your child.

If you and your ex partner share the care of your child between you, then the allowance can be divided between you both.

If you live with the father of your child but are not married to him then you can choose which one of you is going to claim the additional personal allowance.

You cannot claim any other tax allowances in relation to children. You cannot even claim the cost of child care as a work expenses allowance because child-care costs are not regarded by the Inland Revenue as being costs which are 'wholly and necessarily incurred' for your employment.

How can I find out if I am getting my allowances?

You should be told this by the Inland Revenue. If not, you can find out what your tax code is from your pay slip if you are employed. The letters at the end of the Tax Code number indicate which allowances you are receiving.

They are:

H = married man or one-parent family

L = single person or working wife

BR = basic rate. This means that you are not receiving any allowances but are paying tax at the basic rate. It
may be because you are doing two jobs and your tax
allowances have been used with your first job.

F = negative tax code. This means that you are
paying a higher rate of tax.

T = This a a 'neutral' code. You can ask for it if you
do not want your employer to know that you are a single
parent. Your employer might guess that you have asked
for that code because you are a single parent, so it may
not be that effective. Lots of people who are not single
parents have a T code, however.

The numbers in the tax code show the amount of tax
allowance with the last digit removed. For example, the
allowance for a single parent claiming the single person's
allowance and the additional personal allowance for the
tax year 1988/89 was £4095. The tax code would be 409H.

Can widows claim any special tax allowances?

Yes. In 1980 a widow's bereavement allowance was introduced. It is an additional tax allowance paid in the tax
year of your husband's death and for the following year.
For 1989/90 it is £1590. The tax position of a widow is
as follows:

Year 1: In the year of your husband's death:

(a) Your husband will have received the married
man's tax allowance until the date of his death.

(b) You will have been entitled to the wife's earned
income allowance if you were earning until the date of his
death.

(c) After that date you will get a single person's allowance for the full year, the widow's bereavement allowance

and an additional personal allowance if you have dependent children.

Year 2: You will continue to get all these allowances.

Year 3: You will be treated as a single person and will get the single person's allowance plus the additional personal allowance if you have dependent children.

If you are receiving a State widow's pension this is taxable.

Widowers cannot claim any additional tax help, but are, of course, entitled to be treated as a single parent if caring for children. The inequality in treatment may have to change in the future.

What happens to the tax allowances when my husband and I separate?

While you are married, your husband gets a married man's allowance and you get a wife's earned income allowance if you are working. These allowances cease from the date of your separation. After that date you will receive a full single person's allowance for the whole year and also the additional personal allowance if you have children living with you. You should continue to get these allowances for as long as you are separated and a single parent.

Your husband will continue to get the full married man's allowance for the tax year in which you separate, but he will then lose it unless he 'wholly maintains' you by voluntary maintenance until divorce.

If your husband has kept the children, you will receive a single person's allowance only and he will receive the single person's and additional personal allowance for as long as he has the care of the children.

Do I pay tax on maintenance payments?

The law on tax and maintenance payments changed radically as a result of the Budget of 1988. Two systems now operate. The old system for those who had obtained maintenance orders before March 1988 or who had applied for one before that date, and the new system for those seeking maintenance orders after March 1988.

Here the new system is described. The basic position is that there is now very little tax benefit attached to maintenance payments. Where a spouse pays maintenance under a court order or deed to a separated or divorced partner, the paying spouse can claim tax relief on those payments of up to £1590 per year. In effect, this means that a husband will continue to receive the equivalent of the married man's allowance. If a spouse pays maintenance to his or her children, or to a partner for those children, there are now no tax allowances for this. On the other hand, the spouse or children to whom the maintenance is paid do not have to pay any tax on it. It does not count as taxable income in their hands.

Example:
Jane White looks after the two children of her marriage to Robert White. They are divorced and a maintenance order was made on 1 July 1989.
Jane receives as income:

Part time earnings	£5,000
Maintenance for self	£2,000
Maintenance for children	£3,000
	£10,000

Her taxable income consists of her earnings only, as the maintenance is not taxable. Her taxable income is therefore £5,000. Her tax allowances are:

Personal   £2,785
Additional personal   £1,590
                                                  ————
                                                  £4,375

Therefore she will pay tax on £5000 − £4375 = £625
Tax @ 25% of £625 = £156

Robert White will receive a single person's allowance
(£2785) and tax relief on £1590 of the maintenance that
he pays to his wife.

What is the position if my maintenance order was made before March 1988?

The old system applies and the relevant tax reliefs can be
claimed at the rates that existed as at March 1988.

The old system was basically as follows: where a
husband paid maintenance to his wife under a court order
or deed, he could claim tax relief on the whole of the sum
paid. It worked like this. The husband paid the wife the
amount of the maintenance order less tax. He claimed tax
relief on that amount and remitted the tax deducted from
the payment to the Inland Revenue. The wife did not
have to pay any further tax on the maintenance as it had
been paid by the husband. She had to obtain a certificate
of deduction of tax from the husband to prove this. If the
wife was not liable to pay any or all of the tax deducted
because her income was too low, then she could reclaim
some or all of the tax deducted from the Inland Revenue.
This rather complicated system was modified in the case
of certain small maintenance orders which would be paid
to the wife without deduction of tax. The same rules
applied to maintenance paid to children.

The system is rather complex and if you have an old
maintenance order you should seek advice about your tax
position.

Example:

Anne Brown has a court order, made in January 1988, for maintenance of £3,500 per year after tax for herself and for £2,000 per year for their child William from her divorced husband James.

Her income is £3,500. Her tax allowances in 1987–8 were £3795 (single person's and additional personal tax allowances). She is therefore not liable to pay tax and she can reclaim the tax that was deducted from her maintenance before payment to her by James.

William can also reclaim the tax deducted from the maintenance paid to him as the amount is less than the single person's allowance for 1987–8 (£2,425).

James can claim tax relief on the £3500 and £2000 paid to Anne and William.

All can continue to claim relief at these levels (they will not rise) for as long as the maintenance obligation continues. Tax relief will not be available on any increase in the order made after March 1988.

In the above example, Anne will have to get a certificate of deduction of tax from James showing how much tax he deducted from her maintenance before paying it over. She must then give this certificate to the Inland Revenue to reclaim all or part of the tax deducted.

The above applies only to orders made before March 1988.

What happens to my tax if I stop work?

If you have been working and have just stopped, you may be entitled to a tax rebate. This is because, if you are employed, your employer will spread your tax allowances over the tax year and allow a proportion against your taxable income each week or month. If you leave work before the end of the tax year you will not have used all your tax allowances against your pay.

Single parents, who are not required to sign on as

available for work in order to receive income support, can claim a tax rebate after four weeks, and each month after that, to the end of the tax year.

If you start a new job, you will have to give your new employer the P45 tax form that your previous employer completed. This form shows how much tax had been paid in your last job. Your new employer should be able to calculate how much tax you should now pay, and pay any tax rebate due to you. If there is a delay in working out your correct tax code you may be placed on an emergency tax code. This usually means you pay more tax than you are liable for, so it is worth while putting pressure on the Inland Revenue to sort out the correct code quickly.

If you claim or have claimed unemployment benefit, you must remember that it is taxable, so it will be counted in your annual income if you restart work. Income support is not taxable.

Can I get tax relief for housing costs?

You are allowed to claim tax relief on some of the mortgage interest paid on the loan for your home. At the time of publication the limit is £30,000. The amount of tax relief is deducted from your mortgage payments by the bank or building society. This is called the MIRAS scheme (mortgage interest relief at source). It means that you pay a lower amount each month in your repayments to the bank or building society.

If your mortgage is more than the MIRAS amount, you cannot claim any tax relief on the excess.

B. SOCIAL SECURITY

Trying to work out what benefits to claim is always confusing. The social security system changed fairly radically in April 1988 and it is possible that there will be further changes. Do check that the information here is

still up to date and get further help from one of the
organizations listed in Chapter 9.

If I am working and get pregnant, what can I claim?

The lump sum payment of £25, previously paid to all
pregnant women, has been abolished as from April 1987.
This was originally intended to provide help with buying
baby equipment. Now this help is available only to those
who are in receipt of income support or family credit. If
you or your partner are in receipt of these benefits you
can apply for a sum of £85 towards the cost of baby
things. Apply to the DSS at any time after the 29th week
of pregnancy, but not later than 3 months after the baby's
birth. If you have capital of over £500, the grant will be
reduced pound for pound.

You can apply for statutory maternity pay, a new
scheme which came into force in June 1987. You will be
entitled to it if:

(a) you have been working for the same employer for
at least twenty-six weeks by the fourteenth week before
the expected date of your baby's birth, *and*

(b) you have paid National Insurance contributions on
your earnings for the last eight weeks.

Statutory maternity pay is a weekly payment paid by
your employer to you for up to eighteen weeks. Tax and
National Insurance contributions are deducted from it.

You can claim statutory maternity pay whether or not
you intend to return to work. You receive the money once
you have stopped work. Within certain limits you can
choose when to stop work and start to receive the pay.
However, you must give your employer three weeks'
notice that you intend to stop work.

You must give up work, at the latest, by the sixth week
before the baby is due in order to receive the whole
amount of the money. It does not matter if you were

slightly wrong about the date of your baby's birth, you should still receive the full amount.

The basic rate of statutory maternity pay is currently £36.25. If you satisfy certain conditions you can get a higher rate. The conditions are:

(a) you must work over sixteen hours per week for the same employer, *and*

(b) you must have completed two years' service with that employer by the fourteenth week before the baby is due, *or*

(c) you must have worked between eight and sixteen hours per week for the same employer for five years;

(d) you must have earned an average of at least £43 per week.

You will receive 90% of your basic pay for six weeks as higher rate maternity pay. After the six weeks you will just receive the statutory maternity pay at the basic rate noted above.

What if I don't qualify for these benefits?

It may be that you have not worked for the same employer for long enough to qualify for the statutory maternity pay. If so, you may be able to claim statutory maternity allowance. You must satisfy the following conditions:

(a) you must have worked for at least twenty-six of the fifty-two weeks ending with the fourteenth week before your baby is due, *and*

(b) you must have paid full rate National Insurance contributions for twenty-six of the fifty-two weeks.

Statutory maternity allowance is a weekly payment, currently of £33.20, for up to eighteen weeks, paid by the DSS. It is not subject to tax or National Insurance contributions.

In order to claim the full eighteen weeks you must stop work by the sixth week before your baby is due.

Once you have had the baby you will be entitled to child benefit and single-parent benefit (see below), as well as additional tax relief (see page 59).

Are benefits in kind available when I am pregnant?

At the moment all pregnant women and mothers can receive free dental treatment and free prescriptions for up to one year after the birth. Pregnant women receiving income support can get free milk and vitamins.

I am a widow. Can I claim any special benefits?

Yes. There are three benefits to which a widow might be entitled. Entitlement to them all depends upon your husband having made the necessary National Insurance contributions during his lifetime. It is also necessary to show that you were lawfully married to the deceased at the time of his death. Widows' benefits are not payable if the widow remarries or if the widow is cohabiting with a man as husband and wife.

Widow's payment

A lump sum of £1000 is payable on widowhood to women under pensionable age. It is non-means-tested, but the husband must have made the minimum National Insurance contributions in the year before his death.

Widowed Mother's Allowance

This is a non-means-tested weekly allowance payable to widows entitled to child benefit in respect of any child of her late husband or for whom he was responsible. The benefit will continue until the youngest child over 16 leaves school. Your husband must have made the minimum National Insurance contributions, which are similar to the contributions necessary to qualify for a retirement pension. The amount is the same as the basic retirement pension, with additions for each dependent child. It is payable irrespective of any earnings paid to the widow.

Widow's Pension
Widows who are over 45 at their husband's death, or who cease to be entitled to the widowed mother's allowance when they are over 45, are entitled to a widow's pension. The same contribution conditions apply as in the widowed mother's allowance and there is no earnings rule. The amount payable depends on the age of the widow, those under 55 receive less that those over 55. Entitlement ceases at 60 when the retirement pension is payable.

Can I get financial help in respect of the children?

The main benefit related to children is child benefit. It is paid to anyone who is responsible for a child in this country who is under sixteen years old. It is also payable where the child is between 16 and 19 years old but still in full-time education.

It will normally be paid monthly unless, as a single parent, you ask for it to be paid weekly. It will normally be paid to the mother (who is given priority) or to the parent with whom the child is living. This means that if the parents live together the payment will normally be made to the woman.

Your child's temporary absence abroad will not prevent your claim.

You receive a payment for each child who qualifies.

The current amount is £7.25 per week for each child.

Children whose parents are in receipt of income support can claim free school meals, and free milk can be claimed for children up to 5 years old.

Is there any addition for single parents?

Yes. If you are receiving child benefit for a child or children and you are a single parent then you will be entitled to an additional payment on top of your child benefit. It is currently £5.20 per week. You can get only one payment, however many children you have. You have to be on your own with your children and not live with your husband or any other man as his wife.

If you have left your husband you will have to be apart for at least thirteen weeks or obtain a legal separation or divorce before you will be considered as a single parent.

If your husband is absent temporarily or is in prison or hospital, the DSS will not consider you as a single parent. If, however, you can show that your separation is intended to be permanent, you should make a claim and appeal against their decision if they refuse you. Do get advice about how to appeal.

A male single parent can also claim one-parent benefit under the same conditions.

I look after children who are not my own; what can I claim?

You can claim child benefit for a child who is not your child but whose parents are dead or lost, provided you are not acting as a local authority foster parent. You may also be entitled to a guardian's allowance, which is a weekly payment of £8.95 for each child that qualifies. You must be entitled to child benefit in relation to the child on the conditions noted above. You also qualify if the only parent has been sent to prison for at least five years.

Can I get help with school costs?

If your child stays on at school or college after sixteen years of age, he or she may qualify for an educational maintenance allowance from the local education author-ity. It is important to check what your local scheme is and how you qualify as they differ around the country.

You can get help from the local education authority

with fares to school for children of any age, provided your child has to travel more than three miles (if over eight years of age) or two miles (if under eight) to school. From some local education authorities you can get help with the cost of school uniform if your child has to wear one. The schemes will vary from area to area and so you must find out what help your local education authority will give you.

What are the basic benefits provided for me if I am not working?

There are two basic benefits. You can claim either unemployment benefit or income support, depending on how recently you gave up work, your National Insurance contribution record and your financial resources.

Unemployment benefit

This is a non-means-tested benefit paid to those who are unemployed and seeking work for a period of up to one year after the unemployment began. You must have a valid National Insurance contribution record. If you left your job voluntarily you may be disqualified from unemployment benefit for up to 26 weeks. You cannot receive unemployment benefit if you are in full time education or training or in receipt of any training allowance. You must be prepared to accept any suitable job. This may cause problems to single parents who will be able to accept a job only when they have made suitable child-care arrangements. If you are refused benefit on this basis, seek advice immediately. Unemployment benefit is currently £34.70 per week, with £8.95 for each child.

Income support

This replaces the old supplementary benefit. It is a benefit which is means-tested and is not dependent on any National Insurance contribution record. It is the basic benefit available to those who are not employed and who are not entitled to unemployment benefit. To qualify for income support you must:

(a) live in the UK;

(b) be aged over 18;

(c) be unemployed. As a single parent you can still claim, however, if you work part time, for not more than 24 hours a week;

(d) be available for work. But this condition does not apply to a single parent caring for a child under the age of 16, nor does it apply to those caring for an invalid receiving an attendance allowance. If you do register as available for work you will be asked what arrangements you have made for the care of your children if you were offered a job. Work out before you go to the job centre what arrangements you would need to make;

(e) pass the means-test (see below).

If your income exceeds a certain amount you will not be entitled to income support. Nor will you be entitled if you have savings of over £6000.

The income limit depends on the amount you are entitled to claim. A lone parent is entitled to:

Lone parent allowance	£20.80	(under 18)
	£34.90	(over 18)
Child 0–10	£11.75	
11–15	£17.35	
16–17	£20.80	
18	£27.40	
Family Premium	£6.50	
Lone parent premium	£3.90	

In addition you will be entitled to your mortgage interest payments. However, only 50% of those payments will be paid for the first 16 weeks of your income support. Other housing costs can be covered by housing benefit (see page 79).

If your resources fall short of the amount to which you are entitled under the above formula, then you get the balance as income support. In calculating any earnings you have, tax, National Insurance contributions and 50% of pension contributions are deducted. Single parents can also deduct £15 of their earnings. Most other income is fully taken into account, e.g. maintenance or other benefits such as child benefit. Profit from a lodger is also taken into account, but only 20% of what the lodger pays to you is regarded as profit. Where any of your children have income, this will be taken into account in assessing the total amount of benefit you get. However, if the income is not maintenance and it exceeds the amount allowed for a child in the table above, then it will be disregarded, but no benefit will be payable for that child.

Example:
Sarah Jenkins has two children, aged 7 and 11. Her husband has left her. She has a part-time job working 15 hours per week and earning £20 after deductions. Her husband gives her £30 per week for the children and she gets £14.50 child benefit, plus £4.90 one-parent benefit. She has savings of £1200 in a building society. The rent on her council house is £30 per week.

Her resources are:	
Earnings less £15 disregarded	£5
Maintenance	£30
Child and OPF benefit	£19.70
Total	£54.70

Her entitlements are:

Lone-parent allowance	£34.90
Family Premium	£6.50
Lone-parent premium	£3.90
Child under 10	£11.75
Child of 11	£17.35
Total	£74.40

Her capital (and any interest on it) will be disregarded. Her housing costs will be covered by housing benefit (see below).

Deduct £54.70 from £74.40 and the result – £19.70 – is payable as income support.

If I get income support, will I have to get maintenance from my husband?

No, you won't be required to do this. If you get maintenance for yourself or the children then it will be fully taken into account in calculating your income support (and any other means-tested benefit you might be entitled to, such as housing benefit or family credit). This also applies to unmarried partners in respect of maintenance for children.

If you do not ask your partner for maintenance then the Department of Social Security (DSS) may want to do so themselves, under what is known as the liable relative procedure. This means that they will try to agree with your partner a sum he should pay in maintenance and they will collect it. If he will not agree they can take him to the magistrates' court for an order.

You cannot be forced to reveal the identity of your children's father to the DSS if you don't want to.

I get a small amount of maintenance, but it is irregularly paid. Will this affect my benefit?

Yes, it will still be taken into account. This obviously will cause you problems. The best solution to this is to sign over your maintenance order to the DSS. They will then receive the payments from your husband or partner, and also follow up any arrears. They will pay you the full amount of the benefit to which you are entitled whether or not your partner has paid them the maintenance each week. This saves you much bother and uncertainty.

Sometimes my husband gives me or the children a present. Will this be deducted from my benefit?

Not always. Gifts of up to £250 per year from 'liable relatives' are disregarded, and so are 'payments in kind', such as items of furniture or equipment or clothing. Sometimes if your husband pays a bill for you, such as HP instalments, this may be disregarded at the discretion of the benefit officer. Payment of regular bills, such as electricity or gas, will probably not be disregarded.

Can I get help to buy furniture or with other major items of expenditure?

The law on this has changed radically since April 1988. It was possible before then for people on supplementary benefit to get single payments for exceptional needs. Now this system has been swept away and replaced with a system of loans, and some grants, from a social fund.

Two kinds of grant are still available. They are maternity and funeral grants. Maternity grants of £85 are available to a pregnant woman on income support (see page 66). Grants for funeral expenses in certain circumstances are also available.

There are two other ways of getting help from the social fund. One is to apply for a community care grant and the other is a budget loan.

Community care grants are grants, not loans, paid to those on income support in order to assist them to establish themselves or maintain themselves in the community. They are all discretionary and there is no legal right to any of these grants; it depends on the decision of the social fund officer. The Social fund officer is instructed to give priority to certain vulnerable groups of people. Mostly these concern the sick, the handicapped, children coming out of care or ex offenders. Families under stress are also regarded as a priority group. In particular, under this heading, priority should be given to needs arising after a relationship breakdown for removal expenses, a lump sum payment known as a start up grant (of £500) to cover needs for furniture and equipment, and a payment for necessary clothing arising as a consequence of domestic violence. Any capital you already have over £500 will reduce the amount of a community care grant.

The guidance given to social fund officers in making these grants is long and complex. It is best to seek help, e.g. from a social worker of from your local Citizens' Advice Bureau, in making your case.

Budget loans are, as the name indicates, loans intended to help meet important intermittent expenses for which it may be difficult to save from income support. A loan will be made only if you have been on income support for 26 weeks. The loan will be for an amount between £30 and £1000. Any capital you have exceeding £500 will reduce the loan. The loan is repayable over a period of a maximum of 78 weeks by deducting payments from your income support or from other social security benefit payments. Deductions will normally be at a rate of 15% of income support payments per week, but may be less if you have other loans to repay such as hire purchase debts, in which case repayments will be at a rate of 10 or 5%.

Social fund officers are instructed to prioritize applications in the following manner:

High priority	essential furniture and equipment
	bedclothes where stocks are inadequate
	essential removal charges
	fuel meter and reconnection charges
	non-mains fuel costs
Medium priority	non-essential furniture and equipment
	redecoration
	hire purchase and other debts
	clothing
Low priority	rent in advance for non-essential move
	non-essential removal charges
	leisure items

Loans can also be given where a crisis, such as flooding or fire, occurs. These can be granted to all, not just people on income support.

There is no formal appeal against the refusal of a grant or loan, but there is an internal review procedure if you are dissatisfied with the decision.

Can I appeal against a decision to refuse me benefit or reduce my benefit?

You have the right to appeal against a decision on eligibility for benefit made by the DSS except for decisions relating to the social fund. You should put your appeal in writing within twenty-eight days of getting a decision. The case will be heard before an independent Social Security Appeal Tribunal. There can be a further appeal on a point of law to the Social Security Commissioners. You may want to get help if you decide to appeal.

Can I claim any benefits while I am working?

Yes. As noted above, as a single parent you can claim income support even if you work, provided you work less than 24 hours per week and your requirements exceed your resources.

You may also be able to claim family credit, which now replaces family income supplement and is specifically designed for those on low incomes with family responsibilities. In order to claim it you must:

(a) be resident in Great Britain,

(b) be in remunerative work for at least 24 hours per week,

(c) be responsible for a child under 16 or between 16 and 18 and in full-time education. The child must live in your household.

You then have to satisfy a means test. If your capital exceeds £6000 you are not entitled to family credit. If it is between £3000 and £6000 then it is assumed to produce income at a set rate.

If your income is less than £54.80 then you will get maximum family credit (see below). If your income exceeds £54.80 then you will get maximum family credit less 70% of the amount by which your income exceeds £51.45.

> Maximum Family Credit is:
>
> | | | |
> |---|---|---|
> | Adult (single person or couple) | | £33.60 |
> | Child | Age 0–10 | £7.30 |
> | | 11–15 | £12.90 |
> | | 16–17 | £16.35 |
> | | 18 | £23.30 |

You will not get any family credit for a child if that child has capital of over £3000 or if the child has unearned income (e.g. maintenance) which exceeds the amount of family credit for that child.

In assessing income, earnings are taken into account less tax, National Insurance contributions and half the pension contributions. Maintenance is taken fully into account, whether for children or parent. Other social security benefits are normally taken into account with important exceptions – child benefit, one-parent benefit, housing benefit, and attendance and mobility allowances.

If you do child-minding, your profit will be counted as income and will be assumed to be one third of your net earnings. Twenty per cent of income from a lodger is assumed to be profit and therefore counts as income.

Family credit lasts for 26 weeks once it is granted, whatever your change in circumstances during that time. After 26 weeks a new application has to be made.

What help can I get with my housing costs?

Owner-occupiers get help with their mortgage payments either through tax relief on mortgage interest or, if in receipt of income support, as part of that benefit (see page 72).

Tenants can get help with rent from housing benefit which is calculated and paid by your local authority and not the DSS. Go to your local housing benefit office to apply for this benefit.

If you are receiving income support, then you will get all your rent paid by housing benefit. If your income is above income support level, then the amount of housing benefit you may get will depend on the operation of a means test similar to that for family credit. Broadly for each £1 you have over income support level you will lose 85 pence of housing benefit.

If you have capital over £8000, you will not get any housing benefit. Any capital between £3000 and £8000 will be assumed to produce an income of £1 per week for each £250 over £3000.

If you have a lodger or other non-dependent over 18 living in your house, then a deduction will be made from your housing benefit depending on the non-dependent's income and age.

The housing-benefit scheme is complicated and there are many rules relating to who is entitled and how it is calculated. Local authorities are also often slow in working it out and paying it, which may mean you get into arrears. You should seek advice from a local advice or housing centre if you are in any difficulty or there are unusual circumstances in your case.

6: Employment and Further Education

Living on inadequate welfare benefits is not very appealing, although many single parents feel they have little choice. For some, paid work is a necessity and for others a goal to be aimed at once retraining or further skills can be acquired. Many single parents will be in part-time work, or on temporary contracts. They may find that their employers will not give them the benefits granted to non-single parents. You need to be clear about your employment rights and this chapter deals with them and also with opportunities for further education and training.

A. EMPLOYMENT RIGHTS

How do I find out my conditions of employment?

If you work more than sixteen hours a week you must be given written notice of the main terms of your employment. This must be given within thirteen weeks of starting a new job. You will get details of pay, pension rights, holidays, sickness rights, notice and disciplinary procedures. Some of the terms of your contract may be agreed orally between you and your employer and not put into writing. They are still part of your contract.

How much notice am I entitled to?

Generally your contract of employment sets out the period of notice required. However, the law requires certain minimum periods of notice which cannot be reduced by the contract.

If you have been continuously employed by the same employer for between one month and two years, you are entitled to a minimum of one week's notice. If you have been employed for two years you are entitled to two weeks' notice, and then one extra week for each complete year after that, up to a maximum of twelve weeks.

If you work less than sixteen hours a week, there is no prescribed period of notice unless you have worked for at least eight hours a week for five years.

If you have a contract for a fixed term (e.g. two years) then the job will normally last for that period unless the contract says that it can be terminated earlier. The rules on notice will then apply.

If you want to leave you should give your employer at least one week's notice, if you have worked longer than a month. Your contract may specify a period of notice for you. You should be paid during your period of notice.

My employer wants to dismiss me. What can I do to challenge this?

First, if you are a member of a union, consult them. Second, you are entitled to a written statement of reasons for dismissal from your employer. Ask for this; it should be given to you within fourteen days of your request.

You are, however, not entitled to written reasons if you have been employed for under six months, or if you work for less than sixteen hours a week, unless you worked over eight hours a week for five years.

If your employer refuses to give you reasons, you can make a complaint to an industrial tribunal. Once you have the reasons, you can then consider bringing a case to an industrial tribunal.

When can I go to an industrial tribunal?

You can go to an industrial tribunal to get an order that you have been unfairly dismissed (or unfairly declared redundant) and for compensation. You will first have to satisfy the following conditions:

(a) You must have worked for the same employer for 2 or more years.

(b) You must have worked over 16 hours a week, or have worked over 8 hours a week for 5 years with the same employer.

(c) You must be under retirement age.

You have to start the proceedings within 3 months of your dismissal, so it is essential to get good advice quickly. You can consult your union, a local Citizens' Advice Bureau or a solicitor. Legal advice from the latter is available under the legal aid scheme if you qualify on financial grounds (see further on page 111). Legal aid is not available for representation before an industrial tribunal. If the time limit is nearly up and you need to make the application quickly, get the form IT1 from your local tribunal and fill it in. It is not complicated.

You may find that, as a result of your making the application, the arbitration service, ACAS, will seek to get you and your employer to reach an agreed settlement of the dispute. If no agreement can be reached, then the case will go to the tribunal for a hearing. As you cannot get legal aid for a representative at such hearings, you will either have to do it yourself or pay for a solicitor. Your union or an advice agency may be able to provide free representation.

The tribunal will be concerned to find out whether the dismissal was unfair according to the law, and may award compensation if it was. In very rare circumstances the tribunal may order the employer to reinstate the employee. The law in these matters is detailed and complex and cannot be covered within the scope of this book.

I think one reason for my dismissal is that I'm a woman with children. Can I do anything about this?

Discrimination on grounds of sex is illegal under the Sex Discrimination Act 1975. It is illegal to refuse you a job on the ground of your sex, and also to dismiss or fail to promote you on this ground. Discrimination may be direct (e.g. where an employer says 'I won't employ a woman supervisor') or indirect (e.g. refusing promotion to parents and applying the rule solely to mothers and not to fathers). You can bring a case to the industrial tribunal if you have been unlawfully discriminated against. It does not matter how long you have been employed: the restrictions noted above in relation to unfair dismissal do not apply where sex discrimination is involved. It is often not easy to prove sex discrimination and you will need help with the case. Contact the Equal Opportunities Commission or an advice agency. For further information see *The Sex Discrimination Handbook* published in this series.

Can I be dismissed because I am pregnant?

It is unlawful to dismiss you simply because you are pregnant. If you are capable of carrying on working you are entitled to do so and to take available maternity leave. However, some women work in jobs which constitute a risk to themselves or their baby, e.g. where the job involves heavy physical labour or the use of dangerous chemicals. Your employer should seek to move you to work which can be done safely, if this is possible. He or she can fairly dismiss you if it is genuinely not possible for you to do your job while pregnant and there is no suitable alternative work.

However, a claim for unfair dismissal on the ground of pregnancy can be made to an industrial tribunal only if the other conditions already noted are complied with. You must have worked for the same employer for a period of two years, if you worked more than sixteen hours a week. You may therefore find that your employer may take advantage of the fact that you have not been employed for long enough and dismiss you anyway.

Some women have tried to argue (sometimes success-fully) that dismissal because of pregnancy amounts to sex discrimination. As noted above, you do not have to show that you have worked for two years before bringing a claim for sex discrimination. It is worth getting advice on this.

How long can I have off as maternity leave?

You are entitled to a minimum of 29 weeks as maternity leave under the Employment Protection legislation. You must have worked for the same employer for at least two years by the 11th week before the expected date of birth. You must have worked for at least 16 hours a week. Under your contract of employment you may be entitled to more generous maternity leave. It is up to you to decide when you wish to take the leave, e.g. how much you want to take before or after the expected date of birth.

These rights do not apply if your employer is a small employer with fewer than 6 employees and it is not reasonably practicable for him or her to re-employ someone after maternity leave.

What are the conditions for return to work after maternity leave?

If you want to claim maternity leave and the right to return to work, you must give notice in writing to your employer, at least three weeks before you intend to stop work, that you are taking time off for maternity leave and that you intend to return to your job after your period of maternity leave. You must also give to your employer a certificate with the expected date of birth (which the hospital or your doctor can give you). Your contract of employment may also impose conditions where more generous maternity leave is granted by an employer.

Once the baby is born, your employer will probably write to you asking whether you still intend to go back to work. You must reply within fourteen days or you will lose the right to return to work.

At least three weeks before you intend to go back you should again write to your employer stating the date you want to return to work.

If your employer does not offer you your old job but another job, you should get advice as to whether the new job is satisfactory.

You should look to see whether your contract of employment gives you any additional rights.

It is very important to adhere to all these procedures and time limits or you will lose your maternity rights.

You should return to work no later than twenty-nine weeks after the birth of your baby unless your contract or agreement gives you the right to stay away longer.

If you decide not to go back after all, your employer may be entitled to recover some of the money paid to you whilst on maternity leave. This will not be the statutory maternity pay (see page 66), but any additional money that you were paid under the provisions of your contract. Check your contract to see if this applies to you.

Do I have to return to the same job?

In general you have a right to go back to the same job, or reasonably suitable work as favourable as the old job. Some employers may be prepared to offer part-time work or a job-share or more flexible hours to fit in with child care. This is a matter for negotiation with which your union might help. Be careful you do not lose employment rights if you reduce your hours. Job-sharing generally allows a full-time job to be divided between two workers so that between them they cover the full hours. The same terms and conditions should apply to the job-sharers pro rata as would have applied to the full-time post. This may allow you to continue working in your old job when you do not want to work full time. It may be ideal for single parents if the proportion of the salary is high enough to live on.

Can I take time off to look after my child?
Only if your contract allows this. There is no statutory right to parental leave. Some contracts allow for paternity leave around the time of the child's birth for the father of the child or the partner of the mother.

Some contracts give the right to take a certain amount of time off if your child is sick, without having to take annual or unpaid leave.

Can I get tax relief for child care costs?
No. Worse than this. If your employer has a workplace nursery which you use free of charge, the value of this facility is treated by the Inland Revenue as a taxable benefit in the same way as they treat a company car. If you are liable for tax, check the tax implications of accepting a free nursery place.

Who can help organize child care while I am at work?
If your employer does not operate a nursery, then there are the following options.

(i) Childminders
Your local authority Social Services Department registers women who care for children in their own home as child-minders. They check that the child-minder is able to care for children and that she has a suitable home and any necessary equipment. They are supposed to give child-minders support and help sort out any problems. They

may arrange for insurance cover and have an equipment loan scheme. There are recommended rates of pay, and arrangements for holidays and sickness cover. The local authority may lay down guidelines on the number of children to be minded and their ages. Each area operates different guidelines.

Child-minders often mind other children with their own. It is obviously important that you work out whether your needs and those of your child will fit in with the child-minder's own family and needs. It is up to you to sort out your own arrangements with the child-minder, and for you to be sure that you are both happy with the terms you have agreed.

Child-minders are not well paid for the hours and work that they do, but it is a lot of money out of your net income. Some local authorities will help single parents with child-minding costs. As already noted, there is no tax relief for these costs.

(ii) Nurseries

There are some local authority-run nurseries and some private nurseries. They will have different charges and opening hours. Some operate all weekdays, 8.30a.m. to 6.00p.m., and others for just mornings or afternoons. Some will take children of all ages, including small babies, but others will not take children under two years.

Some local authority-run nurseries will reduce the fee if you are a single parent.

It is often extremely difficult to get a nursery place. They are in great demand and often have long waiting lists. Some local authority nurseries may give priority to working single parents, or if you need a break from your children.

(iii) Mothers' helps, Nannies and Au pairs

You may want to employ someone to come to your home

and care for your child as a nanny or *au pair*. Such arrangements have to be made privately and you will be in the role of employer and should think about all the questions like holidays, sickness, tax, etc. There are a number of agencies who help with this, but of course they charge a fee. See Chapter 9 for where to turn for further help.

B. FURTHER EDUCATION AND TRAINING

Single parents often want to do further training or take a course of education. It may well be the stepping stone to work in the future or make up for the further education which was missed earlier because of having children. There are various options available at the moment, and some schemes will allow for a grant or training allowance whilst you are taking the course.

These schemes change rapidly and there may be additional courses in your local area. The library and local job centre should have details of available courses, and your local polytechnic or college of higher education should be able to help.

What help is available if I want to take a degree or other advanced course?

If you already have suitable qualifications or experience you may be accepted to do a course of higher education at a university or polytechnic. Each course will have different rules about the educational qualifications that they demand. It may still be worth contacting the course tutor even if you have not got the exact qualifications. Some colleges encourage older students and will therefore accept students on to the course whom they consider to be suitable, whatever their existing academic qualifications.

Some colleges run a preliminary one-year foundation

or access course for students who have been away from education for some time.

If you have never received a grant for an 'advanced' course before, and the course you are interested in is one that qualifies, you should apply to your local education authority for a mandatory award (grant).

If you and your course are eligible, the grant will cover your fees and provide some assistance with maintenance costs for the whole period of your course – usually three or four years. The amount you receive will depend on your exact circumstances but you should receive additional money because you are a single parent and you have children to support. Some colleges run nurseries for students.

The Department of Education and Science produces a guide to student grants each year and your local education authority should also have information.

The National Union of Students has up to date information on all problems to do with student grants and courses. See Chapter 9 for where to get help.

What training schemes are available?
There are a variety of schemes available for people who are unemployed or who have been out of the labour market for some time. They are organized locally but often run by the Department of Employment.

Most of these courses should be available to single parents but they may not provide child care and so you will have to make your own arrangements for your children to enable you to go on the course.

(i) Employment Training Scheme
This has succeeded the Training Opportunities Scheme (TOPS). It is supposed to provide training and skills courses for you if you have been away from education for two years and are unemployed. The local job centre will

have details. You receive a training allowance while you are on the course and, in certain circumstances, help with child care costs. There are long waiting lists for some courses.

(ii) Wider Opportunities Training Programme
These are wide ranging courses designed for the particular needs of your local area. There are likely to be courses specifically for women wanting to get back into the labour market. Again, the library or local job centre should have details about the courses.

(iii) Enterprise Allowance Scheme
This is specially for someone trying to set up his or her own business. If you are considering doing this but are worried about taking the risk of stopping your income support and becoming self employed, this scheme will pay £40 a week for the first year to help you survive. However, the Manpower Services Commission have to be satisfied that your business venture is suitable and you have to have £1000 capital (which can be raised by a loan) to start.

The local job centre will have details.

What are Adult Education Courses?
There are likely to be a lot of courses run locally provided by the local education authority. Although they charge fees by the session or by the term there are usually reduced fees for people on income support. Some of the courses may provide creche or child-care facilities.

The local education authority or library will have more information.

Can I still receive income support while I am on a course?
Single parents are not obliged to register as unemployed or available for work in order to receive income support.

You can go on a course of study without risking losing your right to income support. If the course has an allowance then you may not be able to receive both payments or they may take the course allowance into account when working out how much money you need in income support. Do check the rules on payment of grants and claiming benefit before you start the course.

7: Divorce, Legal Separation and Maintenance

This chapter looks at the powers of the court to end a marriage and sort out the financial arrangements between couples who have children. The question of housing has already been dealt with in Chapter 1 and custody and access to children in Chapter 2.

It is important to remember that the law treats married and unmarried couples in a different way, however long they have lived together.

A. MARRIED COUPLES AND THEIR CHILDREN

Do I have to get divorced before I can get a maintenance order?
No. You can ask a court to make a maintenance order for yourself or the children as soon as you have separated; and you do not have to ask for a divorce or any other matrimonial order. You can go either to the magistrates' court or to the County court for a maintenance order. These courts are also able to make an order by consent where you and your spouse have come to an agreement about maintenance. A court order when you have already come to an agreement may be useful for tax or enforcement purposes.

How will the court make the order?
Under the Domestic Proceedings and Magistrates' Courts Act 1978, a magistrates' court can make an order for maintenance for you or for your children if your spouse has failed to provide reasonable maintenance.

The court can order that maintenance is paid to you, or

to you for the children or to a child direct. It can be paid weekly, monthly or whatever you want. The court can order that it is paid for a set time, for example for three years only. The court can also order a lump sum of up to £500 to be paid for you or your child.

The court will make the order after looking at all your circumstances, your children's circumstances and those of your spouse. It will have to assess what are your various needs and responsibilities and will take into account your income and that of your spouse. The court will not normally take social security income into account except where the payer is so poor that it would be unrealistic not to do so. The court should bear in mind what it costs to bring up a child.

If the order is for your child, it can last until the child is eighteen, or longer if your child has particular needs.

If you and your spouse have been separated for three months and you have been receiving maintenance, the court can put the arrangement into a court order if you want. If the amount of money you are receiving is not enough the court has the power to increase it.

A County court can make an order for maintenance for your child, but not for you, in proceedings under the Guardianship of Minors Act 1971, if you have applied for and obtained a custody order for your child. The same principles apply, but there is no limit on the amount that can be ordered as a lump-sum payment. However, courts rarely order lump sums for children.

When can I get a divorce?
The court is able to make more elaborate and final orders in relation to both maintenance and property on divorce. In addition you may want the finality of a divorce decree in order to be free to remarry. Full details of the law on divorce cannot be given here (see *The Divorce Handbook* in this series for more detail).

94

Briefly the rules are as follows. You cannot apply for a divorce until you have been married for twelve months. You have to show that your marriage has 'irretrievably broken down'. To show this you must prove one of five facts:

(a) that your spouse has committed adultery and that you find it intolerable to live with him or her, or

(b) that your spouse has behaved in such a way that you cannot reasonably be expected to live with him or her, or

(c) that your spouse deserted you at least two years ago, or

(d) that you and your spouse have lived apart for at least two years and that your spouse agrees to the divorce, or

(e) that you and your spouse have lived apart for five years or more.

There are also other ways of in effect terminating a marriage but they are rarely used compared with divorce. You can apply for a nullity decree which means that your marriage is treated as if it had not happened. You are free to marry as if for the first time. Nullity proceedings are quite technical and have to prove very specific facts to bring a case. You will need legal help. The court has the same powers to sort out your financial and other matters as it has in the case of divorce and will follow the same procedure.

You could also apply for an order of judicial separation. This order does not terminate your marriage, and you are therefore not able to remarry. You show the same facts as in divorce proceedings except you do not have to prove that the marriage is over. The court then has the same powers to deal with your financial and other matters as in the case of divorce. You may want to use these proceedings if you do not believe in divorce or have religious or other reasons which prevent it, but you still need to sort your affairs out and obtain the relevant court orders.

What financial orders are available on divorce?
In divorce, nullity or judicial separation proceedings you can apply for a variety of financial orders.

(i) Maintenance
A maintenance order can be made once the divorce or nullity proceedings have begun as well as at the end of the proceedings, so that you have some regular money coming in pending a final settlement. This order may not be the same as the amount that the court orders at the end of the case.

The maintenance order can order payments to be made at weekly or monthly intervals, or whatever is best for you. The order can be made for you or can be for the children. It may be made payable direct to the child or be paid to you for the child.

The court can also order that payments are secured. This means that trustees control some of your spouse's money or property in case he or she fails to pay the maintenance order. It will obviously only work if your spouse has capital or sufficient assets to provide the security.

(ii) Lump-sum payment
The court can also order a lump sum payment. This can be for any amount, but only one lump sum can be ordered in connection with any one divorce. Nor can it subsequently be varied, so it is essential to be sure to ask for the right amount from the beginning.

(iii) Property
The court will also deal with any property you have, not just the matrimonial home (See Chapter 1 on housing). It can transfer all or some of the property from one spouse to the other.

How will the court calculate the amount of maintenance?

The court will take into account the following factors:

(a) If there are any children under eighteen years old the court must put their welfare first.

(b) The court will then look at your income and any money that you have and the chance of you going to work or increasing your income. The court will also look at your spouse's income.

(c) The court will look at your needs and any particular responsibilities that you have now or are likely to have. The court will do the same for your spouse.

(d) The court will take into account the standard of living that you had when you were together,

(e) your ages and how long you were married,

(f) any disability that either of you have – either physical or mental.

(g) The court will take into account the fact that you may have been at home looking after the home or caring for dependants,

(h) your or your spouse's conduct, but only if it would be wrong to ignore it. The court will not generally take what happened during your marriage into account in working out the financial settlement,

(i) Any loss of pension rights because you will not be a 'spouse' any more.

The court has to take all those facts into account and then try to come up with a settlement which is fair to each of you and provides adequately for the children. Given that there is only a limited amount of money in each family and many families had trouble coping when they were together, it is perhaps not surprising that many court orders are not sufficient to live on.

How long will the order last?

An order for the maintenance of a spouse may last until

he or she dies or remarries. The court can, however, restrict the order for a set period of time, for example three years, and may order that you cannot go back for another order after that time. The court can decide that there should not be any maintenance and make no order.

If the court makes a maintenance order, even if it is for a small amount (of £5 a year for example), you have the right to go back to court to ask the court to vary it if your circumstances have changed. Remember that the court can lower the order as well as raise it.

An order for a child will usually last for as long as that child is at school, but it can be extended if the child stays on in further education or has particular needs.

What happens if the order is not paid?

If you have a maintenance order and it is not being paid, you can apply to the court to have the order enforced. This can be very time consuming and not always very successful.

If your spouse is in regular paid employment, not self-employed, you can apply for an attachment of earnings order if your maintenance is in arrears. This will mean that the employer will have to deduct your maintenance payments from your spouse's wages and send it to the court. The employer cannot reduce the wages below a set amount stated by the court.

If your spouse refuses to obey the court order and fails to pay, you can apply for an order to commit him or her to prison. However, that does not get the money paid.

What happens if we got divorced abroad?

If your marriage has ended by divorce or there have been judicial separation or nullity proceedings in an overseas country, and those proceedings are accepted as proper court proceedings here, then you can apply to a court in England or Wales for a financial settlement. You have to get the court's permission to bring the court proceedings here, but once the permission is granted you are treated just as if you were divorced in this country. However, the courts in England do not have any power to make orders over property that is situated abroad.

B. UNMARRIED COUPLES AND THEIR CHILDREN

Can I get maintenance from my unmarried partner?

A man is not under any legal obligation to a woman with whom he lives or has lived. The fact that you may call yourselves Mr and Mrs Smith does not alter your legal relationship if you are not in fact married to each other. There is no duty to support the other financially. It does not matter how long you have lived together, you cannot apply for maintenance for yourself.

Some couples have drawn up cohabitation contracts which makes provision for maintenance and for the division of property, but it is not clear that a court would hold that the contract was legally binding. This will also apply to couples of the same sex.

Can I get maintenance for non-marital children?

The mother has a legal duty to care for her child and the father has a duty to provide financial support for his non-marital child. The law on this issue changed under the Family Law Reform Act 1987, and this part of the Act is already in force. Prior to this Act, the only way in which the mother of a non-marital child could get a mainten-ance order from the father was by bringing affiliation proceedings in the magistrates' court (no other court was possible). Proceedings had to be brought within three years of the child's birth unless the father had paid money or bought things for the child in that time. Under the new

Act these affiliation proceedings are abolished and non-marital children are treated in the same way as marital children. This means that either parent can bring maintenance proceedings under the Guardianship of Minors Act 1971. The court will be able to award maintenance or a lump sum and make a property order where appropriate. The orders can be secured and the greater enforcement powers of the County courts will be available. Time limits for applications are removed. It will, however, still be necessary to prove paternity where this is disputed.

If the father denies paternity then you will need to produce evidence to the court that he is in fact the father. You may have letters or other things which show that he accepted responsibilities, or friends or relatives might be prepared to give evidence.

The court can give a direction that blood tests should be taken if there is any dispute. These vary in accuracy, according to the prevalence of any particular blood group in the population. Now there are also new blood testing techniques, call 'DNA fingerprinting' which is considered to be 100% accurate. This has been commercially available since 1987 but is more expensive than the old sort of tests.

Can we make an agreement about maintenance?

Yes, if you and the child's father (or mother) wish to draw up an agreement for maintenance rather than go to court you can do so. If the agreement is not kept to, it is possible to try to enforce the agreement or you could take affiliation proceedings.

8: Death and Inheritance

This chapter deals with one of the subjects that often worries single parents – what will happen to their children in the event of their death. There is also the problem of providing for them financially on death and of ensuring that any available property is properly dealt with. There are nowadays fewer differences between married and unmarried parents in this area, but some remain, and so this chapter will deal with them separately. Tax and welfare benefits on death are dealt with in Chapter 5.

A. MARRIED PARENTS AND THEIR CHILDREN

Who has the right to look after my child after my death?

Where parents are married, the person entitled to look after the child on the death of one parent is the other parent. However, either parent can make a will appointing what is known as a testamentary guardian. This person will then exercise parental rights over the child along with the surviving parent. Obviously it is essential to get the consent of the person appointed as guardian; a person cannot be forced to act as guardian if he or she does not wish to do so. If, after your death, your spouse cannot agree with the testamentary guardian about the upbringing of the child then one of them will have to go to court to resolve the issue. The criterion adopted by the court will be the usual one of seeking a solution that is in the best interests of the child.

Of course your spouse also has a right to appoint a testamentary guardian to act with you after his or her death.

Is the position different if I am divorced and have a sole custody order?

Not really. A married parent retains the right to appoint a testamentary guardian after divorce, whether or not a custody order has been made. Similarly the non-custodial parent will have full parental rights on the death of the custodial parent, exercisable along with any testamentary guardian. In one rare situation those rights will not revive on the death of the custodial spouse. This is where, on making the custody order, the court also declares that the non-custodial parent is unfit to have custody (under the Matrimonial Causes Act 1973, section 42). These declarations are rare.

Can a testamentary guardian be removed?

Yes, the court can make such an order. However, it is unlikely to do so in respect of a perfectly fit person appointed by a deceased parent unless there are exceptional circumstances. The decision would be made in the best interests of the child.

What happens if neither parent appoints a guardian?

If both you and your spouse die without appointing a testamentary guardian for your child, then a relative or friend can apply to the court to be appointed as guardian. This is possible only if both parents are dead. If someone else has been caring for your child and you die, but the other parent is still alive, then the carer may need to protect his or her position by applying to the High Court in wardship proceedings (see page 44).

If there is no one to care for your child, then the local Social Services Department will take over the care of your child. Your child may be placed with foster or potential adoptive parents or in a children's home or residential unit of some sort.

B. UNMARRIED PARENTS AND THEIR CHILDREN

Who has the right to look after my child after my death?

The mother alone still has all the parental rights over a non-marital child. This means that the father does not automatically take over parental rights on her death. Only the mother can appoint someone to be the testamentary guardian of her child. The father does not have this right. It is important to draw up a deed of guardianship or a will which will set out what should happen to your child in the event of your death.

On your death the father could apply to the court to be a guardian. He could also apply to act jointly with the guardian you have appointed. The court will have to consider what is best for your child and will make whatever decision is in your child's interests.

Does it make any difference if there is a custody order?

Yes. If the father has legal custody of your child, then he has the right to appoint a testamentary guardian. When the new law under the Family Law Reform Act, 1987 comes fully into force, the father will have a right to be granted joint parental rights with the mother. If this order has been made he will also have the right to appoint a guardian.

C. FINANCIAL ARRANGEMENTS ON DEATH

Should I make a will?

If you make a will you can ensure that your money and property is dealt with after your death in the way you want. It also makes things so much easier for your family or friends after your death. It is even more important if you have a child still dependent on you and so you need to sort out what should happen to his or her financial support.

To make a will you have to be over eighteen years old. A will must be in writing (it can be handwritten, typed, printed, etc.), you must sign it in the presence of two witnesses, and you must understand what you are doing. It is not difficult to draw up a will but there are some legal technicalities that have to be observed, in particular about the signing and witnessing of the will, and some phrases have a particular legal meaning. It is best to get advice or you may end up with something happening which was not what you wanted at all. Advice from a solicitor will not necessarily be an expensive business and if you are a single parent on a low income it may not cost you anything at all as you will qualify for help under the Green Form Legal Advice Scheme (see page 111).

If you decide to draw up a will, make a list of all the money, property and items of value that you have and what you want to happen to each of them. This will make it easier for you to be sure that you do not forget anything and may save some time and money if you are paying a solicitor to help you.

Who should be appointed as executors?
You should also think about who you want to sort out your affairs when you die. These people are called executors and you appoint them in your will to carry out your wishes under it. It is usual to appoint relatives or friends to do this. It is important to check with them that they are happy to do this for you. They must be over eighteen years old. You can appoint your solicitor or bank manager, but remember that they are entitled to charge for doing the work. If for some reason your executors cannot or will not act after your death, the will is still valid. The persons who benefit under the will will have to apply to the court to appoint an administrator of the will.

What happens if I marry after making a will?

If you marry after making a will, this will revoke your will unless it was made with your marriage to your spouse in mind. If the will is revoked it is of no effect at all and if you do not make another will you will die intestate (see below).

What happens if I am divorced after making a will?

Divorce does not, like marriage, automatically revoke a will. It remains valid. However any provisions in the will made in favour of your ex spouse are revoked and that property then counts as 'residue' and will be given to the person named in your will as inheriting anything not otherwise specifically disposed of. This can cause problems and every person who is divorced should ensure that a new will is made to replace the old one.

Can I change my will?

Yes. You can change your mind and destroy your first will and make another one. Alternatively you can add new provisions to your existing will by drawing up a document called a codicil. There are technical rules about destroying or changing a will, so it may be sensible to get legal advice.

What happens if I die without leaving a will?

If you die without making a will, this is called dying 'intestate'. Your money and property should be dealt with according to set rules. The first thing that will happen is that someone will apply for the right to sort out your affairs. The persons so entitled are the following, in order of priority:

(a) surviving spouse,
(b) any children,
(c) father or mother,

(d) brothers or sisters or, if they are dead, their children.

If none of the above exist, then half-brothers or sisters, grandparents, uncles, aunts, or their children if they are dead, can apply to sort out your affairs, provided they have a financial interest in them.

If no one is entitled, then the Crown is entitled to sort out your finances and claim any money.

Only persons who are related to you by marriage or 'blood' can inherit your property on intestacy. If you are cohabiting and are not married, your cohabitee has no right to inherit your property, nor you his. It does not make any difference if you called your relationship a 'common law' marriage or called yourself Mr and Mrs Smith. You may be able to ask the court to make some provision for you from your cohabitant's estate, but you will have to prove that you were financially dependent on him or her (see page 108).

A divorced spouse has no rights to inherit on an intestacy.

Who inherits what on intestacy?
Your spouse has the right to claim:

(a) Your 'personal chattels'. This means cars, household items, jewellery, personal items, but not money or anything connected with any business.

(b) If you leave children, the spouse can take £40,000, with interest at 7% each year until it is paid, and a life interest in what is left.

(c) If there are no children, but a parent, brother or sister or their children, the spouse takes £85,000, with interest at 7% each year until it is paid, and an absolute interest in half what is left.

(d) If there are no children or other relations, the spouse inherits all your estate.

If you have no spouse when you die then the people who can inherit on your death are as follows:

(a) your children,

(b) your father or mother,

(c) your brothers, sisters or, if they are dead their children,

(d) half-brothers or half-sisters or, if they are dead, their children,

(e) grandparents,

(f) uncles, aunts or, if they are dead, their children,

(g) half-aunts or half-uncles or, if they are dead, their children,

(h) if there is no one entitled the Crown will claim your estate.

Can the provisions in my will be changed after my death?

Yes. The Inheritance (Provision for Family and Dependants) Act 1975 allows for certain relatives or dependants to make a claim against your estate if you did not make reasonable financial provision for them in your will, or in the division of the estate according to the rules of intestacy. Obviously you also might have the right to apply for reasonable provision from another person's estate.

You can apply to the court for this provision if you are:

(a) the wife or husband of the deceased,

(b) a former husband or wife who has not remarried,

(c) a child of the deceased. This includes all children whether they are adopted, non-marital or born after the parent dies. A child can apply whatever his or her age and whether or not they have married. However, claims by adults who are healthy and employed and who can maintain themselves may not be successful,

(d) any person who, although not a child of the deceased, was treated as such a child during the marriage.

This means that step-children or other children who may not be biologically related to the deceased can apply for provision from an estate,

(e) any person who was being wholly or partly maintained by the deceased immediately before he or she died. You do not have to be related to the person who died. What you have to prove is that you were dependent on him or her before the death. This would allow for a claim if you lived with someone to whom you were not married. 'Maintained' means that the deceased made a substantial contribution in money or kind towards your reasonable needs. This means that someone like a housekeeper who was paid to look after the deceased is not included.

There may be problems if you and the person who died were dependent on each other, rather than just you being dependent on him or her. If both partners had jobs and contributed equally to the household, then neither will have a claim under the Act for provision from the estate of the other.

What will I receive if I make a claim against the estate of my partner?

If you are the spouse of the deceased, the court will make reasonable provision for you, having regard to all the circumstances of the case. You do not have to prove that you actually need the money for your maintenance. Anyone else making a claim, e.g. an unmarried partner, must show that it is reasonable for them to receive the money for their maintenance so if they are otherwise well provided for they will not get anything. The court will therefore have to consider all your financial and other circumstances.

Can a divorced wife or husband apply for provision?

Yes, but the terms of the divorce settlement might have

removed your right to make a claim under the Inheritance (Provision for Family and Dependants) Act 1975. If you agreed in the settlement not to make such a claim, then you cannot later change your mind and do so. It is the same if the court made an order preventing any such claim.

D. TAX

There are several important facts that you may have to consider if you are dealing with a death. If you have become a widow and/or single parent, then your income tax position will change, see Chapter 5 on tax.

There may also be tax to pay on the estate of the person who died. This can be quite complicated and you may need to seek further advice in preparing the documents for settling the estate for both your purposes and for the Inland Revenue. Depending on how large an amount of money has been left, there may be Inheritance Tax to pay on it. The tax limits change every year so do check that your information is up to date.

9: How to Get Help and Further Assistance

This chapter gives details of where to get more information and advice. How many local agencies there are to help you will depend on where you live, and of course it will also depend on your particular circumstances.

A. ONE-PARENT FAMILY ORGANIZATIONS

National Council for One Parent Families,
255 Kentish Town Road,
London NW5 2LX.
Tel: 01-267 1361.
They began life as the National Council for the Unmarried Mother and her Child and expanded in 1973 to cover all one-parent families – men and women. They provide an advice service by letter or phone on all matters that affect one-parent families, and produce up-to-date information sheets on financial, housing and legal matters which are free to single parents. The advice service is available Mon, Tues, Thurs, Fri, 9.15 a.m. to 5.15 p.m.

They also campaign on issues and welcome information from single parents on particular issues which affect them.

Gingerbread,
35 Wellington Street,
London WC2E 8XF.
Tel: 01-240 0953.
Gingerbread has a network of self-help groups round the country for single parents. Each group may be slightly

different or have different events and aims, but each is run by and for single parents themselves. They may provide practical help in babysitting, after school schemes, evenings out and events for the children. Contact the head office for information about your local group or for help if you want to start a group. They have an advice service at their head office and in some of their regional offices.

Welcare,
(The Church of England Diocesan Board for Social Responsibility),
Church House,
Great Smith Street,
London SW1 3NZ.
Tel: 01-222 9011.
They provide a social-work service for single pregnant women and one-parent families in different parts of the country. They can give advice, counselling and practical help.

B. LEGAL ADVICE AND ASSISTANCE

You may wish to contact a solicitor or get further legal advice about a particular problem. There are local legal advice sessions run by volunteer lawyers in many parts of the country. Sometimes they are organized by the Citizens' Advice Bureaux or by other local legal advice centres. Law centres will have lawyers on the staff and will help people with particular problems who live within their centre's catchment area. Your local Citizens' Advice Bureau, which will be in the telephone directory, will be able to give details.

In addition, solicitors in private practice may take part in the legal aid scheme. This will mean that you will be able to get free advice or advice at a lower fee if you have a limited income. Some solicitors also operate a fixed fee interview scheme where they will only charge £5 for half an hour's advice.

A list of legal aid solicitors is contained in the solicitors' Regional Directory. Each legal aid firm will state which areas of law they cover, but this is no guarantee of excellence. This directory can be obtained from the local library or Citizens' Advice Bureau.

Legal aid and assistance schemes

The Legal Advice and Assistance 'Green Form' Scheme

Under this scheme a solicitor is able to give you advice on any topic of English law and can undertake initial work such as writing letters, making phone calls or drafting documents. The solicitor will calculate whether your income and capital will qualify you for help under this scheme. If you have a low income you may have to pay the solicitor a small fee or you may get free advice. However, if your problem will involve more work or a court hearing the solicitor may have to apply for further legal aid, or ask for an extension of your Green Form cover.

Criminal Legal Aid

If you are charged with a criminal offence you may be entitled to receive legal aid to cover the cost of advice and representation at court. This applies to cases in the magistrates' and Crown courts and will also cover juvenile court appearances. The court will assess whether you need legal aid. They will look both at your financial circumstances and at the nature of the charge. You may have to pay a contribution towards your costs. You cannot receive legal aid if you are prosecuting the offence.

Civil Legal Aid

If you need to defend or bring other court proceedings, you may be able to apply for civil legal aid. The solicitor will have the forms and may help you complete them. The legal aid authorities will need to know about your case and about your financial circumstances. You may have to pay a contribution towards the costs. It can take a long time to process the legal aid application. If your case is an emergency or you need to go to court straight away, your solicitor can apply for an emergency certificate. Until or unless the legal aid certificate is granted, the costs of your case will not be covered by legal aid.

Legal aid is not available for the actual divorce if you and your spouse are not contesting the case, but you can receive legal aid to sort out all the financial and other problems, such as custody of the children and the home. You can receive help under the Green Form scheme to complete your divorce petition.

The Statutory Charge

If you receive legal aid and you recover or preserve money or property in your case, you must check with your solicitor about whether you will have to pay some or all of the costs of the case from your 'winnings'. In many matrimonial cases the costs are not paid by the person who loses the case, they still have to be paid by the winner. If the winner is legally aided, the Legal Aid Board will require the costs to be paid by the winner from the property that has been recovered. They can also put a 'charge' on your home which operates like a mortgage, for the amount of money your case cost. This could mean that if you were to move or sell your home later the Legal Aid Board would have to be paid off from the proceeds of sale. Do check with your solicitor whether this could apply to you. The first £2500 of any property recovered is exempt from the charge.

Useful addresses for legal advice

National Association of Citizens' Advice Bureaux,
Myddleton House,
115-123 Pentonville Road,
London, N1 9LZ.
Tel: 01-833 2181.

Legal Advice Centres and Law Centres: For the local law
centre contact –
The Law Centre's Federation,
Duchess House,
18–19 Warren Street,
London W1P 5EB.
Tel: 01-387 8570.

The Law Society,
113 Chancery Lane,
London, WC2A 1PL.
Tel: 01-242 1222.
(for information about local solicitors who operate the
legal aid scheme – or contact the local library or advice
agency.)

If you wish to complain about a solicitor contact:
The Solicitors Complaints Bureau,
Portland House,
Stag Place,
London SW1E 5BL.
Tel: 01-834 2288.

C. HOUSING

Useful addresses for advice on housing

There are many local housing advice agencies but you
should check whether the advice centre is independent of

the council and whether they will be able to pursue your case for you.

Housing Aid Centres
The Association of Housing Aid produces a directory of centres and can be contacted at: c/o 11 St John's Avenue, Leatherhead, Surrey KT22 7HT. The telephone directory may have the local housing aid centre listed under the name of your local council.

Shelter,
The National Campaign for the Homeless,
88 Old Street,
London EC1V 9AX.
Tel: 01-253 0202.
They may be able to find a local contact who can help you as they have regional workers and provide a national network on housing issues.

SHAC,
The London Housing Aid Centre,
189a Old Brompton Road,
London SW5 0AR.
Tel: 01-373 7276.
They provide advice on housing problems for the London area and produce information on many housing issues. Contact by telephone.

Building societies
There is an association to which many building societies belong. If you have a complaint about a member society contact:
The Building Societies Association,
3 Saville Row,
London W1X 1AF.
Tel: 01-437 0655.

Housing associations

If you wish to find out more about housing associations in your area contact:
The National Federation of Housing Associations,
175 Grays Inn Road,
London WC1X 8UP.
Tel: 01-278 6571.

Women's refuges

There are refuges around the country which will provide assistance to women leaving home because of violence or a threat of violence. Some of the refuges are part of a national network in England and in Wales. Others are independent and some are run by the council. Local advice agencies, Social Services Departments of the local council and the police should know how to contact the nearest one to where you are or where you want to be. The national contact for England is:

Womens Aid Federation,
52–54 Featherstone Street,
London EC1Y 8RY.
Tel: 01-251 6537.

For Wales contact:
Welsh Womens Aid,
38/48 Crwys Road,
Cardiff CF2 4NN.
Tel: 0222-390874.

D. SEXUAL AND RACIAL HARASSMENT

Useful addresses to contact if you have been the subject of discrimination or harassment

Commission for Racial Equality,
10–12 Allington Street,
London SW1E 5EF.
Tel: 01-828 7022.

Equal Opportunities Commission,
Overseas House,
Quay Street,
Manchester M3 3HN.
Tel: 061-833 9244.

National Council for Civil Liberties,
21 Tabard Street,
London SE1 4LA.
Tel: 01-403 3888.

Lesbian and gay discrimination

London Lesbian Line on 01-251 6911 will put you in touch with groups around the country.

Gay Switchboard on 01-837 7324 will also give advice and support and can give you local contacts.

Action for Lesbian Parents,
c/o The Corner Bookshop,
162 Woodhouse Lane,
Leeds LS2 9HB.

Rape

Rape Crisis Centre,
PO Box 69,
London WC1.
Tel: 01-278 3956.

E. CHILDREN

For advice on children's rights

If you want to know more about the rights of your child
you can obtain advice from:
The Childrens Legal Centre,
20 Compton Terrace,
London N1 2UN,
Tel: 01-359 6251.
They will deal with queries by letter or by telephone on all
matters to do with children.

If your child is in care or you want to know more about
your rights and those of your child in the care of the local
authority contact:
The Family Rights Group,
6–9 Manor Gardens,
Holloway Road,
London N7 6LA.
Tel: 01-272 4231.

If you are concerned about problems over custody and
access and want to contact your local conciliation or
mediation service contact:
National Family Conciliation Council,
34 Milton Road,
Swindon,
Wiltshire.
Tel: 0793-618486.

Disabled or sick children

If your child suffers from a particular disability or handicap there are several organizations which may be able to help:

The Invalid Childrens Aid Association,
126 Buckingham Palace Road,
London SW1W 9SB,
Tel: 01-730 9891.
Provides advice to parents of handicapped children.

Mencap,
123 Golden Lane,
London EC1Y ORT.
Tel: 01-253 9433.
Has local groups and regional offices which can give help and support to mentally handicapped people and their families.

Disability Alliance,
25 Denmark Street,
London WC2H 8NJ.
Tel: 01-240 0806.
Provides information on financial benefits available.

National Association for the Welfare of Children in Hospital,
Argyle House,
29–31 Euston Road,
London NW1 2SD.
Tel: 01-833 2041.
Provides a support service and may be able to help with transport and arranges play schemes.

Abducted children

Where the child has been abducted or not returned
contact:
Children Abroad Self Help Group,
Keighley Gingerbread Advice Centre,
33 Barlow Road,
Keighley,
West Yorkshire.

F. NATIONALITY AND IMMIGRATION

There are two main organizations which provide advice
on nationality and immigration questions:

Joint Council for the Welfare of Immigrants,
115 Old Street,
London EC1V 9JR.
Tel: 01-251 8701.

United Kingdom Immigrants Advisory Service,
7th Floor,
Brettenham House,
Savoy Street,
London WC1.
Tel: 01-240 5176.

In addition, the Commission for Racial Equality may be
able to give you some assistance:
Commission for Racial Equality,
10–12 Allington Street,
London SW1E 5EF.
Tel: 01-828 7022.
They will also be able to give the address of your local
Community Relations Council who will be a source of

local support and information. Your local law centre may also take on this area of work and be able to help you. If you consult a solicitor, do take care to ensure that the solicitor is experienced in this area.

G. MONEY

Child Poverty Action Group,
1–5 Bath Street,
London EC1V 9PY.
Tel: 01-253 3406.
They campaign on all questions of welfare benefits and give advice by letter and telephone.

Money Advice Centres:
Contact the National Consumer Council for information about the local advice centre to where you live:
National Consumer Council,
20 Grosvenor Gardens,
London SW1W ODH.
Tel: 01-730 3469.

H. HEALTH

Association for Improvements in Maternity Services,
163 Liverpool Road,
London N1 ORF.
Tel: 01-278 5628.
They have local groups which campaign on issues around pregnancy and childbirth. The national office will put you in touch with a local group.

Maternity Alliance,
15 Britannia Street,
London WC1.
Tel: 01-837 1265.
They provide an information service on all questions for parents and babies, and campaign for improvements in services.

British Pregnancy Advisory Service,
Austy Manor,
Wooton Wawen,
Solihull,
West Midlands B95 6BX.
Tel: 0564-23225.
Advises on pregnancy and abortion. Can put you in touch with a local organization.

Black Health Workers and Patients Project,
259a High Road,
Tottenham,
London N15.
Tel: 01-809 0774.
Campaigns for anti-racist policies in health.

Disability Alliance,
25 Denmark Street,
London WC2H 8NJ.
Tel: 01-240 0806.
Deals with matters concerning disability or handicap.

I. EMPLOYMENT AND EDUCATION

Department of Education and Science,
Elizabeth House,
York Road,
London SE1 7PH.
Tel: 01-928 9222.

Provides information about financial assistance and grants. The local education authority should also have information.

National Union of Students,
457–463 Holloway Road,
London N7.
Tel: 01-272 8900.
Will help with any problems facing students.

Job Centres and local education schemes can be found by contacting the local library or the telephone directory.

Contact the Equal Opportunities Commission or the Commission for Racial Equality for help in cases of race and sex discrimination. See above for addresses.

J. DAY CARE

Contact the local social services department for information about what child care is available in your area.

National Child Care Campaign,
Wesley House,
70 Great Queen Street,
London WC2B 5AX.
Tel: 01-405 5617.
Campaigns for adequate child-care provision for all children.

National Childminding Association,
8 Masons Hill,
Bromley,
Kent.
Tel: 01-464 6164.

K. WOMEN'S RIGHTS

Rights of Women,
52–54 Featherstone Street,
London EC1.
Tel: 01-251 6577.
Provides legal advice for women by telephone three evenings a week – Tuesday, Wednesday and Thursday 7–9pm. It also campaigns for improvements in the law and has a lesbian rights worker.

L. PRISON

Single parents may have relatives or friends in prison or may be sent to prison themselves.

The Women Prisoners Resource Centre,
Room 1,
Thorpe Close,
Ladbroke Grove,
London W10 5XL.
Tel: 01-968 3121.

Prisoners' Wives Service,
75 Marsham Street,
London SW1.
Tel: 01-222 0331.

M. BEREAVEMENT

Cruse,
Cruse House,
126 Sheen Road,
Richmond,
Surrey TW9 1UR.
Tel: 01-940 4818.

Provides advice, support and counselling for all widows and widowers. The national office will put you in touch with a local group.

N. HOLIDAYS

SPLASH,
19 North Street,
Plymouth,
Devon PL4 9AH.
Tel: 0752-674067.
They arrange holidays for single parents.

Holiday Care Service,
2 Old Bank Chambers,
Station Road,
Horley,
Surrey RH6 9HW.
Tel: 0293-774535.
It is a charity which can provide information about holidays for single parents or other groups who have difficulties in arranging a holiday. They do not arrange the holidays themselves.

Local authority social workers may also know of local holiday schemes and may also help some single parents raise the money to pay for a holiday. There are some holiday schemes for children without parents.

Notes

Notes

Notes

Notes

Notes